COINS
& CURRENCY

BRENDA RALPH LEWIS

RANDOM HOUSE · NEW YORK

ACKNOWLEDGMENTS

The publisher would like to thank the following for their invaluable help in preparing this book: Spink & Son, of St. James's, London SW1, for the loan of coins and banknotes for studio photography; Colin and Simon Narbeth, and Philip Cohen Numismatics, both of 20 Cecil Court, London WC2, for the loan of banknotes and coins respectively; Patrick Dean of the Tower Mint Ltd., London SE10, for permission to reproduce the ECU set on page 66; Spink & Son Modern Collections, Croydon, Surrey, for assistance with the maps; and the following individuals and organizations for supplying the pictures used in this book (unless stated otherwise, the photographs in this book were taken specially for Reed International Books Ltd. by David Johnson):

Bank of England 32 bottom left. The British Library 60 bottom (inset). Reproduced by Courtesy of the Trustees of the British Museum 21 top left, 25 top center, 30 center, 36-37 bottom, 37 top left, 37 bottom, 38 bottom left and bottom center, 39, 40 bottom right, 44 top and center, 45 right, 47 top left, 50-51, 53 center left and center right, 53 bottom right, 54 center right, 54 bottom, 55 top, 56 bottom, 57 center, 62 bottom left, 63 center right, 64 left, 65 right, 68 left, 68-69 bottom, 69 top left, /© The Chartered Institute of Bankers 30 top. Peter Clayton 23 bottom left, 24 bottom center and bottom right, 25 top left, 25 bottom left, 29 bottom, 41 bottom center, 59 top. Glendining's 28 top. Robert Harding Picture Library 9, 11, 58, 59 bottom, 61. Michael Holford Photographs 21 right, 24 bottom left. Hulton Deutsch Collection Limited 20 top. The International Stock Exchange Photo Library 8. Biblioteca Medicea Laurenziana, Florence/Donato Pineider 20 bottom. The Board of Trustees of the National Museums & Galleries on Merseyside (Liverpool Museum) 60 bottom (background). By kind permission of the Royal Mint 10, 28 center and center left, 29 center, 69 top right. Thomas de la Rue & Company Limited 32 bottom right, 33 bottom left. B.A. Seaby Ltd./P.F. Purvey 22, 23 top and bottom right, 24 top. Spink & Son 28 bottom, 30-31 top, 37 top right, 54 top and center left, 65 top.

Illustrators:
David Ashby (Garden Studio): 35, 59, 61; Peter Bull Art: maps (72-75).

Editor: Andrew Farrow
Designers: Anne Sharples, Mark Summersby
Series Designer: Anne Sharples
Production Controller: Linda Spillane
Picture Researcher: Caroline Hensman

First American edition, 1993

Library of Congress Cataloging in Publication Data
Lewis, Brenda Ralph.
Coins & currency / Brenda Ralph Lewis. — 1st American ed.
p.   cm. — (Hobby handbooks)
Includes index.
Summary: Includes a history of coins and paper money, covering how different kinds of money are made, forgeries, how to find and identify coins, handling and trading, and how to display a collection.
1. Coins—Collectors and collecting—Handbooks, manuals, etc.—Juvenile literature.
2. Paper money—Collectors and collecting—Handbooks, manuals, etc.—Juvenile literature.
[1. Coins—Collectors and collecting.   2. Paper money—Collectors and collecting.]
I. Title.   II. Title: Coins and currency.   III. Series.
CJ81.L53 1993
737.4'075—dc20   92–46359

Manufactured in Great Britain

1 2 3 4 5 6 7 8 9 10

ISBN 0-679-82662-9 (trade). — ISBN 0-679-92662-3 (lib. bdg.)

CONTENTS

COINS AND BANKNOTES

It is often said that archaeology, the science that discovers the past, is "history in your hand." The same is true of coins and banknotes, or paper money. There is, of course, a direct link between coins and archaeology. Archaeologists have often uncovered hoards of coins lost or buried long ago.

THE WORLD OF COINS

Finding buried treasure is not the only way coins and banknotes can be exciting, though. As a collector, you will be able to own and handle coins that were used by many people before you. A really old coin, such as a coin of ancient Rome, comes to you from many centuries in the past, when great events you can only read about in history books were actually happening. You can never know the people who lived through these events, but you have a link with them: The coins in your hand were once in theirs.

THE BEAUTY OF MONEY

Coins and banknotes are money — they represent the wealth of their owner. These pieces of metal and sheets of paper are used to buy goods and services. But they are also much more than that. Coins and notes tell stories about famous people, great happenings in the past, or great achievements, such as Christopher Columbus's voyage to America. Coins and banknotes can be beautiful works of art, too. Both can teach you something about the countries that issued them. And they depict all sorts of fascinating subjects, such as animals, transportation, plants, maps, and sports.

Anything that people accept as having value can be used as money. Since before the first coins were made, gold (above) has been considered valuable — so valuable, in fact, that it has to be protected in huge bank vaults.

This is money from all over the world. The two forms you find most often are coins and banknotes. As you can see, banknotes look beautiful. Coins come in many different sizes, and they are not all round.

READ ALL ABOUT IT

The purpose of this book is to send you on an exciting journey into the world of coins and banknotes. It tells you how to start your very own collection, how to care for it, how to find out about coins and banknotes, and where to buy them. There are also sections on famous and unusual coins and on the areas of the world that issue coins and banknotes, maps to help you locate these areas, and a glossary of special coin words. There is a lot for you to discover, and we hope you get from it all the thrill and pleasure the world of coins and banknotes has to offer.

Today, people can get paper money from their bank accounts by using automatic machines. They insert a card in the machine, then key in a personal identification number (PIN) and the amount they want. After checking the number, the machine gives them the money.

OBTAINING COINS AND NOTES

This coin dealer is helping a young collector choose a coin and is giving him information about it. Dealers often have enormous amounts of information about the coins and banknotes they sell. They are usually willing to share their knowledge with you. From time to time, very big coin fairs are held in large towns. Dozens of dealers attend these fairs, and there is often an exhibition of coins and banknotes as well.

The coin dealers stand behind their tables, with their stock spread out in front of them. There are small boxes of coins priced at a few cents each. More expensive coins are laid out on trays. Some are Roman, Greek, or other very old coins. Others are more modern and come from all over the world. The dealers are also selling catalogs and books, boxed sets of proof (new and uncirculated) coins, and albums and boxes of banknotes.

AT THE MARKET

This scene is very familiar to collectors who regularly visit coin fairs and markets. To them, the dealers' tables are like "goody bags," packed full of interesting items, perhaps with a surprise or two included. This is the real fun of markets. You may come with your list of coins or banknotes you want to buy, but you never know what else you may find. Maybe a coin you have been seeking for a long time; maybe something you did not know about.

You have to get up very early to go to a coin market. Dealers are usually set up and ready to trade at seven in the morning, or even earlier. By lunchtime, they may have already packed up and gone home. Coin and banknote shops, of course, have larger and more permanent displays of coins and banknotes, and they are open at the same time as other shops.

An auction catalog tells you about the coins and banknotes on sale at the auction. If you want to see them for yourself you can go to the viewing. This takes place before the auction starts. Here you can see the items described with an estimate (the amount on the right) of what the auctioneers think they will sell for.

SPINK COIN AUCTIONS

First Empire, Napoleon I (1804-14)

187   Proof 40-Francs, AN13 (1804-05), A (Paris mint), engraved by Tiolier. Bare head to left, NAPOLEON EMPEREUR. Reverse: value in wreath with REPUBLIQUE FRANÇAISE around and date below. Edge: DIEU PROTEGE LA FRANCE. Weight: 12.881 grams.   £1,000-1,250
Brilliant mint state and extremely rare..

* Sold at Vinchon, Paris 11 February 1963 (No 170).

188   40-Francs, 1806 A (Paris mint). Types as lot 187. Weight: 12.857 grams.   £120-150
Good very fine.

* Sold at van Kuyk, Schulman, Amsterdam 5 June 1961 (No 656).

189   Proof 20-Francs, AN13 (1804-05), A (Paris). Types as lot 187. Weight: 6.449 grams.   £400-600
In brilliant mint state.

* Sold at Vinchon, Paris 9 March 1970 (No 208).

Francs, 1806 A (Paris). Types as lot 187. Weight 6.441 grams.   £100-125

dam 5 June 1961 (No 657).

GETTING THE KNOWLEDGE

Shops and markets do have one important thing in common, though. Both are places where you can meet other collectors and talk to them and the dealers. It is not like going to school to learn set subjects. By looking at coins and notes, checking them in catalogs, reading about them, and hearing what collectors and dealers have to say, you will just pick up the information as you go along.

Look for unusual forms of money. This young Kenyan woman is carrying her money on her head. She can use the gold trinkets to buy goods in a market.

AUCTIONS

At auction, each "lot" of one or more coins is sold to the person who bids, or offers to pay, the most for it. The bidding can be very exciting as several collectors battle for possession of a lot they all want but only one of them can have. You do not have to buy anything if you do not want to, but you can still sit there and enjoy the contest.

BUYING COINS AND NOTES

 When you go to buy coins and notes, make sure you take with you a list of those that you already have. Without one, it is very easy to waste money buying the same coins again. Decide the price you reasonably expect to pay, and don't pay more.

 Check coins' condition carefully. Make a realistic assessment of the wear on the design, and judge the value accordingly. Check that very shiny coins have not been polished clean: Polished coins are not worth as much as ones in their natural condition.

 Examine banknotes carefully. If a note is limp, it has probably been washed; if it curls or glistens, it has been ironed. By holding the note up to the light you will see if any creases have been pressed out. These creases can usually be felt between your finger and thumb, too.

 Banknotes may smell old, but don't buy them if they smell funny - they have probably been stored badly, and their condition will get worse after you have bought them. Check that the color of the note is correct and is not faded from being displayed in strong sunlight.

 If you genuinely believe that an item is priced too high, offer the dealer less money for it. Dealers are likely to be optimistic about how much their coins and banknotes are worth!

COLLECTOR'S HINT
When you go to a fair or shop, take a small pocket coin album or set of coin capsules with you. These will hold your purchases safely until you get them home.

MAGAZINES

You can learn a lot about coins and banknotes by reading coin magazine articles and advertisements. Buying by mail from the dealers who advertise is another way of obtaining coins and banknotes. These dealers may ask for payment when you order. This means you send the payment in the mail (it's best to ask an adult to pay by check for you), and the dealer then sends the things you have purchased.

CLUBS AND SOCIETIES

If coins and banknotes interest you, you will soon feel at home at a club. Experienced collectors are usually only too pleased to help younger and less experienced ones. At clubs, members meet to talk about and look at coins, and they exchange or buy them from each other. Exchanging is a particularly good way of obtaining new coins and notes. It also means you don't have to pay for them with money.

Your local library is usually the best place to find out about clubs in your area. This information is in the reference section. If your school has a coin club you can join it. If not, why not start a club yourself? Larger clubs may have guest speakers to talk about different aspects of the hobby, and there may also be displays, exhibitions, and competitions.

SLABBING

Slabbing is intended to be a precise method of valuing and describing the condition of coins. It is widely used in the U.S. and has become more common in Europe. A dealer assesses the coin's condition and then seals or "slabs" it in a transparent folder. The folder also contains the exact details of the coin's grading (quality).

Many dealers do not accept the system of slabbing. One reason is that slabbing puts a great deal of emphasis on condition and quality when valuing coins, even for older coins that are very rare or that were not minted to today's high standards. As a result, some coins can be valued too highly.

The condition of coins is described in the following manner (just a few of the grades are listed here):

Proofs		Uncirculated (Mint State)	
Proof 70	Perfect	MS 70	Perfect
Proof 65	Choice	MS 65	Choice
Proof 60	Proof	MS 60	Uncirculated

Degrees of wear

AU 50	About Uncirculated
EF 45	Choice Extremely Fine
EF 40	Extremely Fine
VF 20	Very Fine

This slabbed coin (right) is an 1821 British crown graded MS 65. This means it is an Uncirculated coin in Choice condition (better than most Uncirculated coins).

Magazines print articles about coins, notes, and other related subjects (such as cards used to pay for telephone calls), list clubs and their activities, tell you the dates and places of fairs and markets, and carry dealers' advertisements. Look at postage-stamp magazines, too, because some of them include coin information. Catalogs can be very costly, but you can borrow them from your local library.

COIN AND NOTE CONDITION

The condition of coins and notes is of importance to collectors. There's not much point in collecting a poor-quality note if it is widely and cheaply available in very good condition. However, you might be happy to have a poor-quality note if you know it is very rare. Here are some guidelines to help you when you are buying coins and notes. Look carefully at the descriptions — in coin collecting, "Good" means bad!

DESCRIPTION	COINS	BANKNOTES
FDC	Perfect, beautiful condition.	The term is not used.
Uncirculated	Has very fine scratches from knocking against other coins during manufacture.	A perfect, unblemished note — crisp, with only very slight signs of use.
EF or XF (Extremely Fine)	Very little if any wear on the coin.	Has a blemish, otherwise is perfect.
VF (Very Fine)	Small but not important signs of wear, mainly on the raised surfaces.	Undamaged, but may have several folds or other signs of use.
Fine	A bit more worn — the higher points of the surface are worn away — but still a good coin to buy.	Has folds, small stains, wear, but is still attractive.
Very Good	Definite signs of wear, with the detail not good; probably worth buying, all the same.	Has small tears, stains, or pinholes.
Good	Lettering and design are still visible, though the coin is noticeably smooth all over. The date is just readable.	Badly damaged, has bits missing, but the design is complete.
Fair	Very badly worn, date probably not readable.	Worse than Good; has damage to the design.
Poor	Even worse than Fair. Is chipped or pierced.	Awful. Severely damaged.

Uncirculated

Very Fine

Fair

Extremely Fine

Fine

STARTING A COLLECTION

You may want to start collecting because you have a relative who collects, or because you just like the look and feel of coins and banknotes. If you travel abroad, you may want to make a small collection of the coins from the country you have visited, as a reminder of your holiday. However, you have to start somewhere and decide what you want to collect.

LOOSE CHANGE

Look at the small change you have in your purse or pocket. Maybe there is an older coin there. In Great Britain, for instance, you may find a King George VI two-shilling piece, or florin, which you received instead of a more common 10-pence piece of the same size. In the United States, if you're lucky, you may find an Indian-head coin. If it looks interesting, why not keep the coin instead of spending it?

The half dollar (right) and dollar (below right) are collectable coins in the United States. Collecting one coin from each year of issue, particularly the "Indian-head" coins, is popular in the U.S. Collectors living in other countries can do the same. Coin collecting is international, which means you do not have to live in a country to collect its coins.

EQUIPMENT

You will need very little equipment to start your hobby. The only items that are expensive are coin and banknote albums (see pages 34-35); you may already have everything else you need in your home!

TWEEZERS

A few collectors like to use tweezers for picking up coins, so that dirt and perspiration from their hands don't damage the coin. If you decide to use tweezers, buy ones that have coated ends — bare metal ends will scratch the coins.

ADDING TO THE PILE

If you keep enough coins, you will soon have the start of a collection. Or rather, you will have a mixture of coins that needs to be turned into a collection. So the next thing to do is to find out about other coins that go with the odds and ends you have already.

At this stage, learn all you can about coins by reading books on the subject, looking at catalogs, or joining a coin club. For now you have an important decision to make. There are too many coins for you to collect them all. So you are going to have to specialize in some of them. But which ones?

MAGNIFYING GLASS

You will need a magnifying glass to look at the fine details of coin and banknote designs. A pocket magnifying glass can be useful when you visit shops. If you want to look closely at a coin, make sure the glass does not scratch the coin.

USING A CATALOG

Catalogs look complicated, but they are easy to use. First, read the introduction to the catalog, which will explain how the information has been arranged. Then, using the index, find the country or region whose coin or note you want to read about. The coins might be listed in date or value order. The prices given in catalogs are usually for Very Fine, Extremely Fine, and Uncirculated conditions. Fine coins may be worth even less than these values. A typical catalog entry for Maltese coins is shown below.

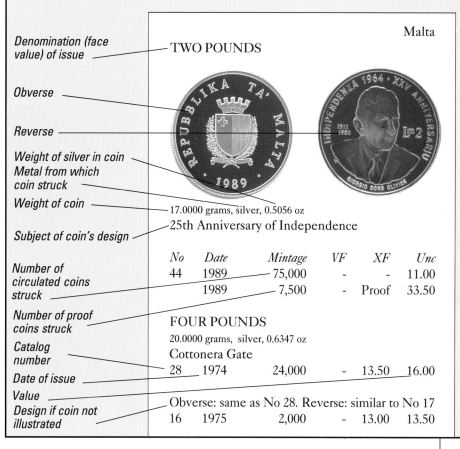

Malta

Denomination (face value) of issue — TWO POUNDS

Obverse

Reverse

Weight of silver in coin
Metal from which coin struck
Weight of coin — 17.0000 grams, silver, 0.5056 oz

Subject of coin's design — 25th Anniversary of Independence

No	Date	Mintage	VF	XF	Unc
44	1989	75,000	-	-	11.00
	1989	7,500	-	Proof	33.50

Number of circulated coins struck

Number of proof coins struck

FOUR POUNDS
20.0000 grams, silver, 0.6347 oz
Cottonera Gate

| 28 | 1974 | 24,000 | - | 13.50 | 16.00 |

Catalog number
Date of issue
Value
Design if coin not illustrated

Obverse: same as No 28. Reverse: similar to No 17

| 16 | 1975 | 2,000 | - | 13.00 | 13.50 |

Here are coins and notes from the reign of King George VI (1936–1952). There were two kinds of threepenny coins in general use: a small silver one (1937–1944) and the 12-sided nickel-brass threepenny (1937–1948). Also shown here are four silver Maundy coins — one-, two-, three-, and four-penny pieces, given each year by the monarch in a special ceremony for the poor.

WHAT TO COLLECT

Because coins have been used for some 2,600 years, the choice of what to collect is enormous. It is the same with banknotes, even though they have been issued for only a quarter of that time. The choice is huge even if you leave out the rarer items that you will not be able to afford.

If you become interested in an American Indian-head coin or British George VI florin, for example, you could go on to collect more coins of the United States or Great Britain. However, there are lots of other ways to decide what your collection will contain. You may be interested in the country your family came from; you may have relatives living abroad. Or you like the coins of a country you have visited on vacation. You could collect the coins of that country, and the banknotes too, if you wish.

JUST ONE COIN

It can also be interesting to collect lots of examples of the same coin. There is something very pleasing about seeing coins that were issued over a long period of time all lined up in year order in an album or coin box. Luckily, this kind of coin can be quite cheap to buy, because it was usually minted in large numbers. The more coins of the same design there are, the lower the price you have to pay for each one. The same goes for banknotes.

You can also make an interesting collection from coins struck to commemorate, or remember, special events (see page 42). For example, the Olympic Games and soccer's World Cup are held every four years, with countries from all over the world taking part. That means commemorative coins are issued all over the world, too.

Whatever you decide to collect, the most important thing is that the subject both interest and please you. The best collection is one you will enjoy reading about and looking at.

THE RIGHT SUBJECT

Before you start your collection, do some research in catalogs and books. Make sure that you haven't chosen too big a subject, or one that will be very difficult to complete because the items are very rare and expensive. There's nothing worse than spending time and money on a collection you cannot develop to its full potential.

You could start a collection from any of these coins. They are, top to bottom: a Belgian five-franc coin issued from 1986 on; a 10 cents (1958–1979) from Hong Kong; a Portuguese 50-centavo coin (1927–1968); a Ceylonese cent (1963–1971), one of the last coins produced by Ceylon before it changed its name to Sri Lanka in 1972; a French two francs, first struck in 1979; and a Canadian "voyageur" dollar, first issued in 1936.

COLLECTING BY THEME

Do you have a particular interest in, say, animals or aircraft or maps or some other subject? Lots of coins can be collected by theme — though if you choose automobiles as a subject, you will not get very far. Only one coin, a 1928 silver dollar from China, has ever depicted a car, and it is very expensive, too — over $650 in Extremely Fine condition. Otherwise, you have a very wide choice: Subjects such as sailing ships, space exploration, elephants, lions, trees, fruit, music, famous people, and many more have all been depicted on coins. Here are some subjects that can be used as themes.

An ox on a 50-butut coin of 1971 from The Gambia.

A bird on a 50-cent coin of the British Virgin Islands.

Flowers on a 1970 Canadian dollar.

A ship on a 10-escudo coin from Portugal.

A volcano (right) on a 1964 50-cent piece from the Philippines.

A space shuttle and launch rocket on a Marshall Islands five-dollar coin.

The Olympic Games are held every four years. Here are commemorative coins from Mexico (1968), Germany (1972), Poland (1980, for the Soviet Union's games of that year), and Spain (1990, for the Barcelona games of 1992).

WHAT CONDITION?

Experienced collectors usually buy coins that are Very Fine or better. You might not be able to afford the prices of some of the top-condition coins, and so may have to accept coins as low as Fine. However, it is better to gradually build up a collection by buying a few top-condition coins at a time than to rush out and buy lots of coins in poorer condition. If in doubt, don't buy. In years to come, you will appreciate a collection of top-condition coins more than one filled with poorer ones. Be patient!

COLLECTING BANKNOTES

Although banknotes (paper money, or bills) have not been issued for as long as coins, you can, in time, get together quite a large collection of them. Many thousands of banknotes have been printed in the last 200 years as more and more paper money has replaced or supplemented (been added to) metal money. Countries such as Mexico and Costa Rica, in Central America, and China and Hong Kong, in Asia, have issued very large numbers of banknotes. Most of these are relatively inexpensive to buy, as well as very attractive and colorful.

This 1949 banknote (above) comes from the Mediterranean island of Malta. The cross on the note represents a bravery medal, the George Cross. During World War II, Malta suffered many air raids. Afterward, its people were awarded the medal as a tribute to their courage.

A JOB LOT

Because there are so many countries and banknotes to choose from, the best way to begin collecting is to buy a job lot from a shop or fair. A job lot is a large quantity of notes, sold together at one, usually not too high, price. It contains about 50 or 60 notes and gives you a wide range from all over the world.

Next, choose a few notes that you find particularly appealing. Then read catalogs and books to find out about the sets and themes (see next page) they belong to. Now you can decide what you want to collect.

When you buy a job lot and spread them out to look at, this is what you will see: plenty of color, interesting designs, skillful engraving, and lots of information. Remember, though, that job lots usually contain only common banknotes, ones that have been produced in large quantities.

COLLECTOR'S HINT
When you start your first collection, choose only low-denomination notes in Very Good condition or better. Leave the higher-denomination and rarer notes (which will be more expensive) until you are a more experienced collector.

The "White Fiver" of Great Britain, as this £5 banknote (right) is called, is one of the most famous of all notes. It was issued until 1957.

The colorful banknotes below are *Notgelden*, a German word meaning "money of necessity," or emergency money. They were issued in 1920, during a period of tremendous inflation in Germany. This means prices went sky-high, and money lost its value. Prices rose so quickly that goods had to be re-priced twice each day.

This is a Hell Note (left), imitation paper money issued in China. Hell Notes were burned on funeral pyres, because the Chinese believed that dead people needed money in the afterlife.

SETS AND THEMES

Banknotes often come in sets, a group of notes issued at the same time. So, if you have one note in a set, find out about the rest. Banknotes also carry interesting pictures — famous people, animals, ships, or trains, for instance. These usually tell you something about the country that issued the notes. From all this, you can decide what you want to collect: the banknotes of a certain country or area of the world, or banknotes with themes or subjects that interest you — or even banknotes of the world, as long as you can afford the time and money required.

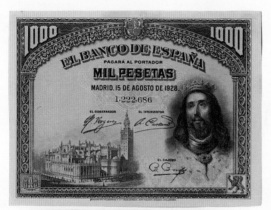

These banknotes issued by Spain in 1928 depict famous Spaniards such as the painter Velázquez (50 pesetas) or Cervantes (100 pesetas), the author of the popular novel *Don Quixote*.

BARTER

Our modern money is so important to us, to buy the things we need or want, that it is hard to imagine a time when it did not exist. The 2,600 years that coins have been used may seem an enormous length of time, but human beings have lived on Earth far longer than that. So how did they obtain what they needed before they started using coins?

NO NEED FOR COINS

In the so-called Stone Ages, people hunted animals for food. They used animal skins for clothing, and bone, stone, or wood to make weapons and tools. They also picked berries and leaves to eat. They did not need money, because the Earth's animals and plants provided everything they needed to live. These ancient hunter-gatherers were usually nomads. This means they did not have fixed homes, but wandered about, following herds of animals from place to place.

BARTER

Much later, though, some people settled down in one place. Some became farmers, some kept animals, and others made tools and weapons. In other words, people began to specialize in the work they did. And in order to buy food, clothing, or other items, they bartered. Barter, in which one thing was exchanged for another, was the oldest form of trading.

At first, the goods exchanged were animals, food, and skins. This is how many "money" words we use today originated: they were words to do with animals. For example, "pecuniary" means "about money"; it comes from the Latin word *pecus*, meaning a herd animal. The salaries people get for their work originated with the *sal*, or salt, which Roman soldiers sometimes received as pay. Basically, people bartered with goods they grew or made but did not need — the surplus of what they had produced.

In the 15th and 16th centuries, when European traders first traveled to Asia and America, they traded by barter with the people they met there. In the Molucca Islands (in what is now Indonesia) the inhabitants grew cloves, nutmeg, and other spices, which Europeans wanted to flavor or preserve meat. This picture shows a trader offering lengths of cloth in exchange for the spices.

In ancient Mexico, the Aztecs used bands of red feathers or cacao beans as small change. Most of their trade, though, was done by barter. This picture from the Codex Florentino, an old Mexican painted book, shows merchants with some of their barter goods, including jewelry, pots, feathers, and a jaguar skin. They also traded in mantles, or cloaks.

20

The ancient Egyptians did not use coins or currency, but traded by barter. However, they did use rings as money. This scene, from an Egyptian tomb, shows money rings being weighed (top left).

In 1981 and 1982, China issued postage stamps showing many kinds of barter goods: knives, shovels, and cowrie shells. Bronze coins were made in the shapes of these objects in China before 221 B.C. Their values were usually based on the coins' weights. Most of the bronze coins had the name of the issuing city or state inscribed on them, and occasionally the value. Knife and hoe coins were briefly reintroduced from A.D. 9 to 23, although their value was then not related to their weight.

STRANGE MONEY

The early societies soon developed strict rules about the exchange of goods. Gradually, certain items were given a standard value, against which the value of all other items could be measured. In many regions of the world, metals became a recognized form of payment. In Mesopotamia (now southern Iraq), weighed amounts of metal were used; in China, small pieces of bronze shaped like the goods they represented came into use.

Some barter goods may seem strange to us. At one time, people on the Atlantic island of Tristan da Cunha used potatoes for barter. In China and Tibet, people used dried tea formed into bricks. Beads, shells, and feathers, too, were used. However, all these items had one thing in common. They were all recognized by the people using them as being a reliable means of payment.

THE FIRST COINS

The Greeks of ancient times started so many of our modern ideas about art, science, and architecture that it is not surprising to find they also invented coins. It happened in about 650 B.C. in Greek settlements in Lydia, western Turkey. There, archaeologists have found several coins in the Greek cities along the coast, such as Ephesus.

A GUARANTEE OF VALUE

These coins did not look like those we know today. They were egg-shaped blobs of electrum, an alloy (mixture) of gold and silver. On one side of the blob were scratched lines that indicated its weight, and therefore its value. On the other side, a simple mark was punched into the metal. The mark was the personal seal of the person who had guaranteed the weight of the blob. It is from this process of stamping a coin that we get the term "minting." Using these "coins" for payment was a great success.

SILVER AND GOLD

About a hundred years later, coins showed animal designs, including the lion's head which was the symbol of the kingdom of Lydia. At this time, around 550 B.C., the ruler of Lydia was King Croesus. He was famous for his great wealth and was the first, it seems, to mint coins of pure gold and silver.

Before long, silver coins were being used in cities in Turkey and Greece. Some beautiful coins with fine portraits of kings and princes were produced. One of them, a silver tetradrachm struck by King Lysimachus of Thrace in Greece about 300 B.C., carried a portrait of Alexander the Great. It was made so carefully that it is still possible to see every curl of Alexander's hair.

ALEXANDER'S EMPIRE

A few years earlier, Alexander, a brilliant soldier, had conquered a huge empire that stretched as far as India. He set up mints (small factories for making coins) all over his vast territory, and large quantities of gold and silver coins were struck there. The designs were often taken from Greek mythology and showed Zeus, ruler of the Greek gods, or Athena, the Greek goddess of wisdom.

These three coins are from the Greek states. The two gold staters of King Croesus of Lydia (above and above right) have detailed pictures of a lion and a bull. The Ionian coin (left) is one of the earliest known. It is made from electrum, a mixture of gold and silver.

These two coins (left) show Alexander the Great and Cleopatra VII of Egypt. How are they connected? The Alexander coin was struck in about 310 B.C. by Ptolemy I, who set up a kingdom in Egypt. Cleopatra, shown on a coin struck in about 50 B.C., was the last ruler of the Ptolemy family.

After Alexander died in 323 B.C., his generals seized parts of his empire and set themselves up as kings. They struck their own coins, with their own portraits on them. Then, in the 2nd century B.C., Greece was conquered by the Romans. Afterward, Greece was given a new currency. The new coins were the Roman aurei or denarii, the bronze coins used to pay the soldiers of the occupying army.

This very early coin from the island kingdom of Aegina is one of the coins named "turtles." The leather-backed turtle depicted on it was the symbol of Aegina, an important trading center in the 7th and 6th centuries B.C. Eventually, "turtles" circulated in many of the Greek trading posts that had been established around the Mediterranean Sea.

After the Romans conquered Greece, fewer coins were struck, except for bronze coinage. One of the few important coins minted at this time was the famous "owl" coin of Athens shown here. Athens was named after its patron, or protecting goddess, Athena, and for hundreds of years she appeared on Greek coins together with the owl. These "Athena and owl" coins were the first to have a recognizable design on both the obverse (front) and reverse sides.

THE ROMANS

Several empires have existed in Europe over the centuries. However, none was as large and long-lasting as the Roman Empire. At its greatest extent, about 1,800 years ago, the Roman Empire stretched from Britain in the northwest down to the deserts of Arabia in the southeast. It covered most of western Europe and extended into North Africa.

ROMAN REMAINS

Part of this enormous empire lasted until 1453, when the eastern Roman Empire, known as the Byzantine Empire, was conquered by the Turks. It is still possible to see evidence of Roman civilization all over this huge area. Archaeologists have found temples, public baths, roads, and even whole towns where Romans once lived. They have also found Roman coins, sometimes in ones or twos, sometimes in large hoards. People often buried hoards of coins in times of trouble or war, but some never returned to dig them up again (see pages 58–61).

THE FIRST MINT

Surprisingly, for such an organized society, the Romans took quite a long time to start issuing coins. It was not until 269 B.C. that a mint for striking bronze, silver, and gold coins was set up. Before that, the Romans had used lumps of bronze for money, then bronze bars or ingots. In 269 B.C., the mint in Rome began striking heavy bronze disks such as the as, which weighed nearly one pound. At the same time, the mint produced silver coins much like Greek coins; they even had a Greek name — drachma.

This is a silver denarius of 211 B.C., struck in Rome. The denarius was first struck in about 212 B.C., at the time of the Roman Republic. The "X" behind the helmeted head shows the value to be 10 as. The denarius gave its name to the dinars used in Yugoslavia, and also to the deniers used in the Frankish Empire in France and Germany, ruled by Charlemagne over a thousand years ago. Much later, the British predecimal penny was indicated by a "d," after the denarius.

ROMAN EMPERORS

Emperors' faces appeared on Roman coins. Their titles, often in shortened form, will help you identify them. "IMP" stands for *"Imperator"* or *"Emperor."* "PP" stands for "Parent (or 'Father') of the People."

An as of Claudius, A.D. 41–54.

A dupondius of Hadrian, A.D. 117–138.

A sestertius of Nero, A.D. 54–68.

A sestertius of Caracalla, A.D. 211–217.

ROMAN COINS

As time went on, many famous and important Roman coins were introduced. These included the silver denarius (211 B.C.); the gold aureus, introduced by the first Roman emperor, Augustus, who reigned from 27 B.C. to A.D. 14; the antoninianus (A.D. 215), the follis (A.D. 295), and the gold solidus (A.D. 315). Early Roman coins often carried the family names or symbols of the officials who issued them, together with images of Roman gods and goddesses. Later, powerful politicians or generals issued their own coins. Once the emperors came to power, though, only they and their families were allowed to do this.

After the Roman Empire became Christian in the 4th century A.D., the Christian "Chi-Ro" symbol appeared on the reverse of Roman coins (right). The "X" is Greek for "CH," and "P" stands for "R." "CHR" are the first three letters of "Christ."

ROMAN INFLUENCE

Roman designs have influenced coins minted centuries afterward. For instance, the Roman brass dupondius was struck over 1,800 years before this U.S. coin, but both show an eagle on the reverse.

You might not be able to buy many ancient coins because most are rare and expensive, and many are kept in museums. However, some companies make reproductions (below), accurate copies of the coins, to sell to people who want to have an "ancient" coin. Copies usually look new and bright.

As of Antonius Pius

Follis of Constantius I

EARLY DATES

The most famous of all Romans, Julius Caesar, put his age — LII, or 52 — on gold and silver coins which he struck after conquering Gaul (France). These were among the first coins to have anything like a date on them. Caesar was born in 100 B.C., so this coin was struck in 48 or 47 B.C.

Dupondius of Nero

Sestertius of Vespasian

WHAT DO THEY SHOW?

Coins and banknotes are not just methods of paying for purchases. Countries use their coins, as they use their postage stamps, much like advertisements. The coins of a country can depict its famous people, its achievements, its wildlife, and sometimes the scenery and countryside as well.

A MINE OF INFORMATION

A coin or note, even a small one, has to carry a great deal of information. For example, a modern coin may carry the name of the country that struck it, its value and denomination, and the date it was struck. If it is a commemorative (see page 42), the name of the event or person it remembers has to go on, too.

(see page 42)

RIMS AND EDGES

A coin's rim is a ring of raised metal running around the face. Many coins have fine decoration (usually teeth or fine beading) just inside the rim. This is to deter people from cutting metal off the outside of coins to make their own.

The edge of a coin is the side seen end-on. Early hammered coins (see pages 28–29) had plain edges. Milled coins usually have a pattern of fine grooves, called graining.

(see pages 28–29)

Inscriptions (writing) are another form of edge, and have proved very popular. Most coins do not have graining as well as writing. Inscriptions are rare on non-circular coins.

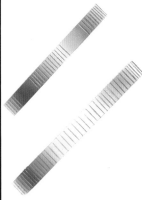

The obverse of this 1879 dollar (far left) depicts the head of Liberty. It also has the date, the motto "E pluribus unum" ("From many, one"), and 13 stars representing the original 13 states of the United States of America. The Canadian dollar (left) cleverly uses the word "river" twice in the title because Canada has two national languages, English and French. "Fleuve" is one of the French words for river.

This 25-øre coin from Denmark, struck in 1984, has a very simple design. The obverse tells you who the monarch of Denmark was at the time: the monogram (letter symbol) M2R with the crown above represents "Queen Margarethe the Second." The reverse shows the country name and coin value.

A WORK OF ART

However, coins and notes are more than just pieces of metal or paper with information on them. Great skill and artistry have gone into making them. They have beautifully made images — portraits, patterns, coats of arms, sometimes detailed pictures of town scenes or of sports being played. Yet the designers of coins cannot use all the space on the coin. Plain spaces must be left so that the image is clear and the coin does not look overcrowded. A design must also be the correct distance from the edge of the coin, where a certain amount of room must be left for inscriptions or titles of, for example, the head of state of the country.

One of the first things a newly independent nation does is issue coins, banknotes, and postage stamps. In 1960 a province of the Belgian Congo declared itself independent, as the Republic of Katanga. This 100-franc note was issued in 1962, the last full year of Katanga's short-lived independence. Today, Katanga is the province of Shaba in southeast Zaire.

MINT MARKS

Many coins, especially those from the U.S., carry a mint mark. This is a symbol, usually a letter or letters, that show where the coin was minted, or struck. You usually have to look carefully for these mint marks, because they may not be obvious when you first see the coin.

The mint mark "M" on this Italian gold 40-lire coin tells you it was minted at Milan, in northern Italy.

FASCINATING NOTES

Banknotes carry more information than coins and stamps, which are much smaller. From a banknote you can identify the country it comes from, the year, the month, and even the day it was issued, the name of the issuing bank, the denomination or value of the note, and its serial number. These are the front and back of a 100-franc note of the West African States, now eight independent states.

HOW COINS ARE MADE

Modern coins begin as designs made by an artist. When the design is approved, it is given to a sculptor, who makes a large model of the coin in clay. Next, plaster casts are taken, and extra, delicate detail of the design might be added, sometimes with fine drills like those used by dentists.

A coin mint about 500 years ago (above). The man in the middle is hammering out a sheet of metal. On the left, the metal is being cut into blanks with shears. On the right, the coinmaker strikes coins, using a pile and trussell. In the background is the master of the mint. The balance on his right was used to make sure blanks were the proper weight.

Coins are inspected regularly to ensure a high standard of production (left). Trial pieces (below) are made on spare metal before minting. These designs were tested but never issued on coins, so the pieces are extremely rare.

An artist works on the design for a coin (above). The design is many times the real size of the coin.

MOLDS AND DIES

The completed plaster casts are made into a nickel mold. From this, a steel cutter transfers the large coin images onto a master die, or hub, of the actual coin size. Then the designs are transferred to a working die. This has to be very hard and durable, because it is from this working die that the actual coins will be struck. So, to strengthen the steel from which it is made, the die is treated with chemicals and heat. The die is cleaned and might also be polished with tiny grains of diamond. A typical die is durable enough to strike at least 200,000 coins.

METALS

Nearly all coins are made of metal. The metal is chosen with several requirements in mind. For example, cheap metals are used for low-value coins, but hard-wearing metals are needed for ones that will be handled frequently. Early coins were made of gold and silver. These metals' main disadvantage is softness. Copper has been used for many low-value coins. Nickel, zinc, tin, and aluminum have been used on their own, but are better as alloys (mixtures of metals), which wear better and are more resistant to staining and corrosion than the pure metals. Steel and iron coins have been used, too, especially in Africa in the 19th century.

Austrian aluminum schilling of 1947.

Danish zinc five øre of 1959.

Stainless-steel 100 lire of 1973, from Italy.

A Malaysian coin produced from tin.

A five rubles from the USSR, with copper-nickel ring and brass center.

HIGH-SPEED PRESS

To make the actual coins, blanks are fed into a high-speed press. Then the coin is struck, and the images on the die are impressed on each side of the blank. Inside, the collar holding the blank in place may be plain or "milled" (with ridges). As a result, the finished coin will have a plain or milled edge.

Proof coins are struck far more precisely than ones for normal circulation. The specially prepared blanks are struck twice using high-quality dies. Many mints issue "proof-like" coins that are not of the standard of proofs; don't confuse the two types.

HUMANS AND MACHINES

For most of the time people have used coins, they made them the hard way: by hand. The earliest Roman coins were "cast," by pouring heated metal into molds. So were early coins made in Japan, China, and Korea, where cast coins were still being made in 1891. In Europe, though, coins were produced by "hammering." A sheet of metal was hammered out and circular "blanks" cut from it. After the blank was trimmed and filed, the impression of the die was struck onto it with a hammer.

The pile (right) held the lower die; the trussell (below) held the upper die. A blank was placed between them. In this way, the hammer struck obverse and reverse designs at the same time.

This Japanese gold koban (right) was made by casting in 1860. After casting, the coin, which was in reality a large thin metal plate, was stamped with four "chop" marks. The Japanese characters painted on in India ink form the mint mark.

PAPER MONEY

People use banknotes instead of, or in addition to, coins, to buy the things they need. Notes are usually printed for larger amounts than coins. Because they are lightweight, notes are much easier to carry around than the same value in coins.

THE FIRST BANKNOTES

The first people known to have used banknotes were the Chinese. Instead of carrying bags of heavy coins everywhere, people began to leave their coins with merchants, in return for a receipt. Then someone had the idea of paying for goods with the receipts instead of the coins. Although the receipts were only paper, they represented real money held by a merchant. Soon the government took over the job of issuing receipts. To make the system simpler, they were printed and issued only in fixed values.

The earliest notes date from A.D. 860, although some collectors believe there were notes in China about 200 years earlier. However, the most famous of the early Chinese banknotes were printed much later, some time between 1368 and 1399, when China was ruled by emperors of the Ming Dynasty. These Ming notes were printed on the bark of mulberry trees. They carried a warning that counterfeiters would have their heads chopped off.

EARLY PROBLEMS

Ming notes were not very successful. In times of war, or when there was inflation and prices rose sharply, they became worthless because people no longer had confidence in their value. People preferred to have their real money. Therefore the early banknotes were abolished, and their use forbidden.

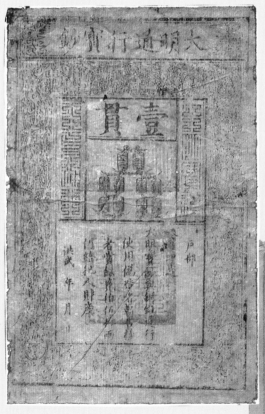

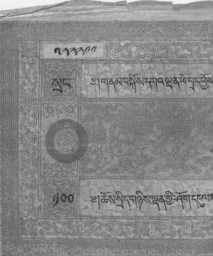

This banknote (left), made in China, was printed on mulberry bark. The 100-srang note from Tibet (below) was issued nearly 600 years later, between 1947 and 1950. Not much had changed, though. The look of the two notes is very similar. The Tibetan note was printed on rice paper, which is made from bark.

PAPER MONEY

Banknotes are promissory notes, that is they are a "promise to pay" the bearer of the note in real money. This Australian banknote of 1905 (left) carries the inscription "We [the bank] promise to pay the bearer here on demand fifty pounds."

This 100-daler note of 1666 (above left) was one of the first European banknotes. It was issued by the Swedish Bank of Stockholm.

When is a postage stamp not a postage stamp? Answer: When it is a banknote. This British South Africa Company stamp was printed on cardboard and used in Rhodesia, Africa. These "banknotes" are known as Marshall Hole currency, from the signature on their obverse.

Banknotes also became worthless if banks did not keep enough coins for when people wanted to redeem, or swap, notes for "real" money, as they were entitled to do. A loss of confidence in the bank could cause people to rush to redeem their notes — the origin of the term "a run on the bank." A "run" could force the bank out of business. For instance, the Bank of Stockholm in Sweden was the first European bank to issue banknotes, in 1661. Unfortunately, these were not supported by the government, and so the bank had to close within a few years.

The first European bank to issue paper money on an official, permanent basis was the Bank of England. It was set up in 1694 to raise money for a war. Within four days, wealthy merchants and others had subscribed (lent) £100,000 to the bank. In return they received handwritten "bank notes." These represented the money they had paid into the bank.

In 1790 the National Assembly of France issued paper money called assignats (above). Too many were issued, and they soon lost much of their value. Pictures on banknotes (below) are not always what they seem. If you turn this German note to the left, then put your finger over the man's face, you will discover a vampire!

The Michigan State Bank note below was never issued: The bank was merged with another bank in 1864.

HOW BANKNOTES ARE MADE

Unlike coins, modern paper money has a life of months, not years. Many countries print millions of banknotes *every day* in order to replace those that are too worn or dirty to be used. Designing and printing these banknotes is a fascinating process that combines many traditional crafts with high technology. All of the work has to be done with great secrecy and security, to avoid forgery.

THE DESIGN

Artists and designers work constantly to produce new designs and features for the notes of the future. Once it's decided that a new note is required, a design is chosen from artists' sketches. The first sketches are usually made with traditional pen and ink. As work progresses, computer-aided design (CAD) equipment is used to draw the complicated patterns that are used on banknotes.

THE ENGRAVER'S WORK

The main picture of the design is still engraved by hand, using very fine tools and powerful magnifying glasses and microscopes. The engraver cuts the design, in reverse, into the printing surface, a steel plate. The cutting depths of the engraving must be incredibly accurate. It can take months to complete a single picture.

PRINTING METHODS

Paper money is printed using two or more methods. The main image on the engraved plate is printed by the intaglio method. This method gives a thick coating of ink but is expensive and cannot be used to make a multicolored design. Usually, the complicated pattern of the background design is printed by lithography. Lithography uses a chemical process to transfer the design to a printing plate or cylinder. This method can be used to print a multicolored image, but a separate plate is needed for each color.

Banknotes must be hard-wearing and have a pleasant, crisp feel. Therefore a special paper with watermarks is used, made from cotton fibers. The printing inks, too, must be chosen carefully: they contain security features to prevent illegal copying and are very expensive.

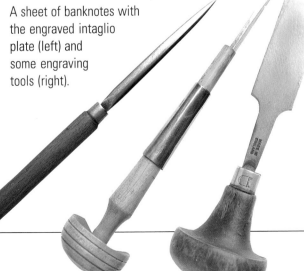

A sheet of banknotes with the engraved intaglio plate (left) and some engraving tools (right).

NUMBERING AND CHECKING

The final printing process is the numbering of the banknotes. The number is different for every note, so it must be printed by a special machine called the letterpress. Signatures are sometimes printed in this way, too.

Banknotes are printed in large sheets, or in a continuous roll (web) which is then cut into sheets. Before it is cut into individual notes, each sheet is checked, by eye, for flaws. A machine cannot do this time-consuming job any better than a person.

Security against forgery is very important in the making of paper money, such as this note from Mozambique. One of the most difficult things to copy is a security thread running through each banknote. Other security features are the watermark in the paper, the bank governor's or government treasurer's signature, and the serial number. Also, the complicated geometric patterns, today produced using computer-aided design equipment, are hard to copy.

Once the design has been printed, a unique serial number is put on each banknote by special numbering boxes mounted on a separate press, which can print 10,000 sheets (each sheet has 32 banknotes) in an hour. The sheets are then checked, and the imperfect notes are marked; they are later replaced. Finally the sheets are cut into individual notes and stacked in serial-number order.

PRINTING METHODS

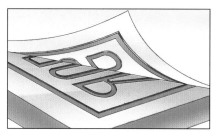

INTAGLIO

In this method, the design is cut into the printing surface. The surface is then inked and wiped, leaving the ink in the engraver's lines. Next, the paper is laid on the plate, under pressure, and picks up the ink of the design.

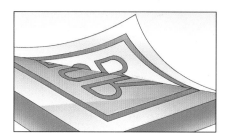

LITHOGRAPHY

Lithography uses a greasy substance to transfer the design to the printing surface. The surface is then moistened and ink applied. Because oil and water do not mix, the ink sticks only to the greasy part of the surface, which then prints the ink onto the paper. Banknotes use a variation of the method called offset litho. The design is first transferred onto a rubber "blanket" which then prints it onto the paper.

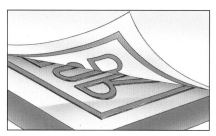

LETTERPRESS

In letterpress printing, the design is engraved, but the areas that are not required to print are removed from the printing surface. The ink is put on the raised surface of the design, and is then transferred directly to the paper.

KEEPING YOUR COLLECTION

You can see how much a collection needs protecting by looking at the dirty and damaged coins or banknotes that dealers sell very cheaply. Many of these would cost a lot more if they were in good condition. Sometimes, of course, you will buy old coins that are worn or scratched because you find them especially interesting or because better examples are too costly to buy. Even so, you should treat these coins the same way as new ones, so they do not get any worse.

It is a good idea to move coins and banknotes around inside plastic pockets like those in this album. This ensures they do not get stuck to the plastic.

ALBUMS

Coins and banknotes should be kept in proper albums, the best ones you can afford. Albums have plastic pages with pockets for each coin or banknote, so that you can look at them from both sides without removing them. Choose a coin album with plenty of rings in the center to hold the weight, because a full page of coins can be extremely heavy. Coins come in many sizes and shapes, so make sure you buy plastic pockets that are the right size to hold each one.

Paper envelopes are a cheap way of protecting coins. They do not last as long as plastic and are not such an attractive method of display. However, you can write details of the coins on the envelopes.

COLLECTOR'S HINT
Store your collection in a cool, dry, and shady place. Damp can do terrible things to coins and notes, and strong sunlight will make the notes fade.

BOXES

Some collectors and dealers do not keep coins or banknotes in plastic. They believe that, in time, some kinds of plastic will cause staining and other damage. They prefer to keep their coin collections in boxes. The boxes have trays covered with a velvety material.

Coins look elegant in boxes. The color of the trays shows them off very well.

Shown here is a good album for paper money. Do not be tempted to display your banknotes in stamp or photograph albums. The paper leaves could damage your collection.

When using a box for your coins, you can give them extra protection by enclosing each one in its own capsule. Capsules enable you to handle the coins without actually touching them.

KEEPING A JOURNAL

Keep a journal about your collection: it will make it more interesting to look at for you and your friends. Tell a story with the coins or banknotes you have collected. Someone seeing your collection for the first time should immediately be able to understand what the collection is all about. Include only simple information for identification, and then additional details that are not obvious from the coin or note. It is also worth keeping a record of what you have paid for items and where you obtained them, for insurance purposes.

DIRTY COINS

Some experts believe coins should never be cleaned. Others feel they can be, but only with special chemicals, not household cleaners or polish or anything that would damage a coin.

RIGHT

To keep them from getting dirtier, only pick up coins if you have clean, dry hands. Hold them by the edge, between your thumb and forefinger.

WRONG

Never touch the faces of a coin, especially a proof one. The sweat from your hands is slightly acidic and will quickly leave a finger mark you will never be able to remove.

THE CARIBBEAN

The Caribbean Sea and its many islands, which lie close to the American continent, have had a very dramatic history since 1492, when Christopher Columbus explored the area during his first voyage to America. It was here that the Spaniards, French, British, and Dutch fought to possess various islands. Some of them, such as St. Lucia, were captured by one or the other several times.

RAIDERS AND SLAVERS
Here, too, pirates and privateers raided settlements and carried off treasure, booty, and prisoners (see p. 59). And thousands of slaves, captured in Africa, were brought to the Caribbean to work on sugar cane and other rich plantations.

This eventful history shows in the coins and banknotes of the Caribbean area. For example, a copper penny of Barbados, minted in 1788, shows the head of an African on the obverse. A copper halfpenny of the Bahamas (1506) depicts a three-masted warship on the reverse; the motto reads (in Latin): "By expulsion [throwing out] of pirates commerce [trade] is restored." The same message appears on a four-shilling banknote issued by the Bank of Nassau in the Bahamas in 1953.

In 1950, British-ruled Caribbean islands, together with British Guiana on the nearby northern coast of South America, joined to use one currency, based on the dollar. The new currency of 1955, like this 50 cents of 1965, circulated in the British Virgin Islands, Anguilla, St. Kitts, Nevis, Antigua, Dominica, St. Lucia, St. Vincent, Grenada, Trinidad & Tobago, Barbados, and British Guiana.

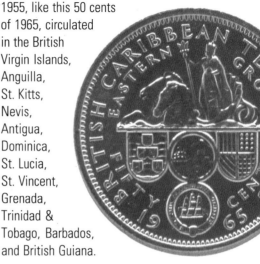

COINS FROM EUROPE
When the fighting for the islands was over, Haiti, which shares the large island of Hispaniola with the Dominican Republic, was held by the French. So were Martinique and Guadeloupe. The Bahamas and Barbados were British, as were Bermuda, the Virgin Islands, Jamaica, Trinidad, and Antigua. Cuba, Puerto Rico, and the Dominican Republic were ruled by Spain. The Dutch had the Antilles.

The first coins in the British-ruled islands of the West Indies, as the Caribbean area is called, were

The two-gourde banknote (right) was issued a century after Haiti won independence from France in 1804. Coins from the Bahamas (left) have designs symbolizing the islands, such as the shell on this 1989 dollar.

Because of a shortage of British coins, this Spanish gold eight-escudo coin of King Ferdinand VI was counterstamped GR, for King George II of England. It was used in British-ruled Jamaica in 1758.

introduced in 1822. Their values were fractions of the Spanish silver dollar: one-sixteenth, one-eighth, and one-quarter. Long before this, though, several islands used counterstamps. These were coins from another country punched with a special mark. The first to use counterstamps was Jamaica, in 1758. French islands such as Martinique and Guadeloupe also started with counterstamps, using mainly Spanish coins. To make small values, some coins were cut into wedges and then each was counterstamped.

This is a quarter-dollar segment cut from a Spanish dollar, minted in about 1800. It is known as a "treble island mutilation" because it has been cut, then counterstamped *three times*. Its obverse was counterstamped for use on the island of St. Vincent. The reverse, shown here, was counterstamped with three "S"s for use on St. Kitts, and later counterstamped again for use on Tortola.

The island of Cuba gained independence from Spain in 1898, but the old Spanish banknotes continued to be used after that. Like this 10-peso note of 1896, these banknotes were issued by the Spanish Bank of the Island of Cuba.

EUROPE

The Vikings, from Scandinavia, were very adventurous sailors. In their longships, they made voyages across the North Sea and into the Atlantic Ocean. In 1979, the Isle of Man remembered the Vikings on a one-crown silver coin (below). In 1957, Iceland, which was settled by Vikings after A.D. 874, issued a five-krona banknote showing a Viking warrior (bottom).

When the western Roman Empire (centered around Rome) disintegrated after about A.D. 476, much of Europe became a wild and dangerous place. Where the Romans had once ruled and people were able to lead peaceful and civilized lives, barbarian tribes such as the Visigoths, Huns, and Vikings terrorized towns and villages, and killed the people or carried them off as prisoners.

BYZANTIUM

The eastern Roman Empire, centered around Byzantium, or Constantinople (now Istanbul in Turkey), survived for another thousand years. The Byzantines, as its people were called, continued the Roman way of life: its cities, its arts, its trade — and its coins. Byzantium also had emperors, and one of them, Justinian I, was the first to put a date on his coins: A.D. 527, the year his reign began.

THE BEZANT

The Byzantines produced gold, silver, and copper coins, many of them in a strange saucer shape. The most important was the gold bezant, which was widely used in Europe and parts of what is now called the Middle East. The bezant had a great influence on European coins at this time. Even the barbarians needed money, and for a long time they copied Roman and Byzantine coins. Like Roman emperors, barbarian chiefs put their own portraits on their coins, together with Roman-style inscriptions.

This is a gold solidus minted in Byzantium. On the obverse, it shows Emperor Leo VI (A.D. 886–912). On the reverse, Leo is shown with another Byzantine emperor, Constantine VII. Double portraits of two emperors or an emperor and his wife appeared on Byzantine coins for over 300 years.

This is a gold thrysma minted in the 7th century A.D. in the Kingdom of Kent in southeast England. Compare it with the Byzantine coin to see how the double emperor design was copied.

This is a silver denier of a 9th-century king of France, Charles the Bald, who was also the Holy Roman Emperor. The denier was named after the Roman denarius.

Like the denier from France (right), these European coins feature the cross of Christianity. The coin below comes from 9th-century Belgium, the one at the bottom from 15th-century Ireland. Missionaries traveled all over Europe converting people to Christianity in the centuries after the end of the western Roman Empire.

THE MIDDLE AGES

As time passed, the barbarians settled down and began to form the countries and regions of Europe we know today. They kept their Roman-style coinage, though. In France, for example, the Merovingian rulers introduced the silver saiga, based on the Roman denarius. In Italy, which was divided into many small states, beautiful gold and silver coins were struck. In the late 8th century, Pope Adrian I, who ruled a territory around Rome that was later called the Papal States, struck the first papal coins. Later popes employed the finest sculptors and medal artists to produce ducats and sequins. In Germany, there was the silver bracteate. In Russia, the princes of Kiev copied Byzantine coins. In England, Anglo-Saxons copied Roman coins. Scandinavian coins copied the Anglo-Saxon types and the German bracteate.

SILVER THALERS

Early in the 16th century, huge deposits of silver were discovered at the St. Joachimsthal mine in Bohemia (Czechoslovakia). The find had a great effect on European currency: the large coins made from this silver circulated throughout the continent. The coin was first called the Joachimsthaler, then thaler for short. Eventually this name was used all over the world. Its most famous modern descendant is the dollar, now used in the United States, Canada, Australia, New Zealand, and elsewhere.

A NEW CURRENCY

The thaler gave Europe a new kind of currency separate from that of ancient Rome and Byzantium. In England, Scandinavia, and other countries, however, the name was changed to "crown." The early Joachimsthalers, minted by the counts of Schlick, who owned the mine, featured a cross and a heraldic shield, or escutcheon. These features gave their name to Portugal's escudo and Brazil's former currency, the cruzeiro. The thaler became most famous in Austria, with the Maria Theresa thaler of 1782 named after the reigning empress of Austria.

Two coins from Italy. The 10 lire at the top is a modern coin of 1974 from the small independent state of San Marino in northeast Italy. Above is a small silver 10 grana of 1818, showing the head of Ferdinand I, from the Kingdom of the Two Sicilies (Sicily and Naples). The kingdom was one of the states that joined together in 1860 to form modern Italy.

MARIANNE

Allegorical, or symbolic, portraits of women often appear on coins. Marianne, a symbol of France, is the figure on this five-franc coin of 1933. Even the Phrygian cap she wears is meaningful. Originally, caps like this were worn by freed slaves in Phrygia, in ancient Greece. In 1789 the French revolutionaries started wearing them after they rebelled against their king, Louis XVI. Thus the picture of Marianne wearing a Phrygian cap symbolizes French freedom from tyranny.

This is one of the famous thalers that gave Europe a new kind of currency. It was issued by Stephen, Count of Schlick.

MODERN COUNTRIES

Since the first silver thalers were issued in 1518, the countries of Europe have changed a great deal. In the past, some of these countries belonged to empires. Hungary, for instance, was once part of the Austrian Empire. Others, such as Germany and Italy, were a mass of small states before they unified (became one country), just over a century ago. Changes are still happening. In 1990, West and East Germany, which were divided in 1945 after World War II, became united as one country again. In 1991, the three Baltic states of Latvia, Lithuania, and Estonia left the Soviet Union and became independent.

A CHANGING WORLD

Changes in countries can, of course, mean changes in coins, so you can follow history in your coin collection. This is one of the features that make collecting the coins of Europe especially exciting. A collection of Italian coins and banknotes, for instance, could start with coins from some of the individual states — such as Venice, Milan, or Lombardy-Venetia — and then show those issued by unified Italy after 1860.

These are coins of West and East Germany, which existed when the country was divided from 1945 to 1990. The coin on the left is the reverse of a two marks of West Germany. Below are both sides of an East German two marks.

These three banknotes are from Norway (top), Estonia (middle), and Eire (bottom), a former name of Ireland.

Here are 12 coins from countries in Europe. They show how the coins' small size makes symbols important.

Maria Theresa thalers (right), named after an 18th-century empress of Austria, are among the world's best-known coins. They were first issued in 1780, and this same date appears on many other thalers even though they were struck much later. The Maria Theresa thaler was also used in the Middle East and in North and East Africa.

COMMEMORATIVE COINS

Today, important anniversaries, events, or famous people are regularly depicted on coins, but the idea is a very old one. Over 2,000 years ago, the ancient Greeks realized how useful coins could be for commemorating events, such as the Olympic Games, which were first held in 776 B.C. In the ancient Greek colony of Syracuse, silver dekadrachms were given as prizes to winning sportsmen. Today, Olympic champions receive medals, but it is easy to see how like coins these medals are.

ANNIVERSARY COINS

The Romans, who took many ideas from the Greeks, copied this one, too. Their most ambitious commemoration was a long series of coins depicting the history of Rome. These were struck in A.D. 348 to mark the thousandth anniversary of the city.

The idea of commemorative coins has continued ever since, though in the 15th century large gold medals took over from coins for a while. One very important event was commemorated twice, by several states in Germany. This was the Reformation, commemorated on its centennial in 1617 and on its bicentennial in 1717. The Reformation was the breaking away of the Protestant from the Catholic church, started by the priest Martin Luther in 1517.

These three commemorative coins (right) are from the United States. The first is a 1982 silver half dollar that celebrates the 250th anniversary of the birth of George Washington. The 1987 silver dollar (middle right) commemorates the 200th anniversary of the American Constitution, which begins "We the people." On the far right is a silver dollar for the 1988 Los Angeles Olympic Games.

This silver 10-markka coin was issued by Finland in 1967 to commemorate 50 years of independence from Russian rule. The obverse shows five swans. The reverse shows building construction, a symbol of the country's progress. Finland was the first country to issue an Olympic commemorative, for the 1952 Helsinki Olympiad.

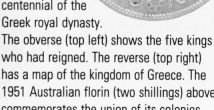

In 1963, Greece issued silver 30-drachma coins for the centennial of the Greek royal dynasty. The obverse (top left) shows the five kings who had reigned. The reverse (top right) has a map of the kingdom of Greece. The 1951 Australian florin (two shillings) above commemorates the union of its colonies.

MODERN COMMEMORATIVES

Commemorative coins as we know them today were first struck in the U.S. in 1893, when a half-dollar and quarter-dollar were produced to mark the 400th anniversary of Christopher Columbus's arrival in America. In Britain, the crown, or five-shilling piece, had not been used since the early years of this century, but it was revived in 1935 as a commemorative coin for the Silver Jubilee (25th anniversary) of King George V's coronation. Since then, crowns have often been issued for special commemorations, royal and otherwise.

Recently, commemorative coins have become more popular than ever before. Some of them come in sets from different countries celebrating the same event. For example, 19 countries struck matching coins after 1968 to celebrate the Coin Project of the Food & Agricultural Organization (FAO) of the United Nations. The idea behind the Coin Project was to let people know about the work of the FAO in improving agriculture and food production throughout the world.

In 1492, Christopher Columbus made his first voyage to the Americas. He first landed in the Bahamas, which in 1989 issued this five-dollar coin to commemorate his arrival. Columbus claimed America in the name of his patron, Queen Isabella of Spain. Columbus wasn't a Spaniard, however. He came from Genoa, Italy. On 500-lira coins first struck in 1958 (right), Italy depicted his three ships, *Santa Maria*, *Pinta*, and *Niña*.

TREASURE ISLAND

Why does a Scottish man appear on a coin from a group of small islands in the Pacific? Robert Louis Stevenson, the author of *Treasure Island*, *Dr. Jekyll and Mr. Hyde*, and many other exciting stories, went to live on Upolu Island in Samoa in 1889. Because of his bad health, he needed the warmer climate Samoa provided. In 1969, Western Samoa issued this one-tala (dollar) cupronickel coin to mark the 75th anniversary of his death.

This 1939 Canadian silver dollar depicts the parliament building in Ottawa, visited in that year by King George VI. First issued in 1935, Canada's silver dollar has often been used to commemorate important national events.

NORTH AMERICA

Compared to some other parts of the world, North America (Canada and the U.S.) was very late in acquiring coins of its own. Coins were not minted for use in North America until 1652, when the British colony at Massachusetts Bay struck some rather rough silver pieces. Canada issued its first coins 18 years later, in 1670.

COINS FROM AROUND THE WORLD

However, before they had their own coins, all sorts of money were used in Canada and the North American colonies. There were French, Dutch, English, and German coins. The Spanish silver dollar, or eight reales, was in use all over the New World, as the Americas were called. There were even coins from China in western Canada, where many Chinese people had emigrated in order to find work, bringing their coins with them.

Tokens, too, were used, especially by fur trappers in Canada, with denominations valued in beaver skins. There was also a barter system in which the "currency" was animal skins and dried fish or, in the U.S., tobacco and wampum (see page 21).

The 10-dollar gold eagle was one of the first coins of the newly independent United States. However, for 60 years after this coin was minted in 1795, there were not enough gold eagles. So, people continued to use the Spanish silver dollar and other foreign currency.

In 1913, the U.S. government established the Federal Reserve Bank system, to issue notes that were "secured by United States bonds deposited with the Treasurer of the United States of America." This meant the notes were properly supported by "real" money and were much more reliable than previous U.S. banknotes.

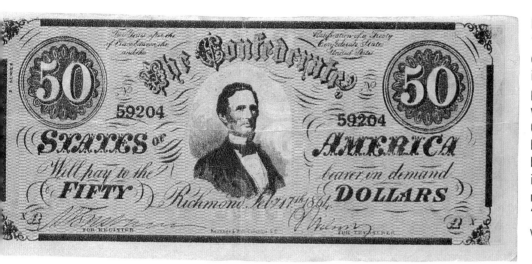

During the Civil War of 1861–1865 the governments of the North and South issued huge amounts of paper money to pay for the war. In the South, the Confederate States' banknotes (left) soon became worthless. Inflation in the North caused their new notes, called "greenbacks," to lose some value, too.

TODAY'S COINS

Nine years after the U.S. won its independence, Congress passed the 1792 Coinage Act, which listed four basic types of coins to be issued: gold eagles, silver dollars and dimes, and copper cents. The designs on the coins had to symbolize liberty, or freedom. This was very important because the U.S., assisted by France, had fought a long, hard war to gain its liberty. This is why the head or the figure of Liberty, an allegorical (symbolic) woman, has appeared on so many U.S. coins. It is still used today, and the types of coin chosen in 1792 are among the currency of the U.S. over 200 years later.

This Canadian silver one-dollar coin was issued in 1958 to commemorate the centennial of British Columbia. The obverse carries the portrait of Queen Elizabeth II of England. Elizabeth II is Queen of Canada and of several other territories in the British Commonwealth.

CANADA

The most common feature of Canadian coinage is the British monarch's head. This is because Canada remained first within the British Empire and later the Commonwealth. Like the U.S., however, the Canadian currency has denominations of dollars and cents.

The Canadian provinces once had their own currencies. The bronze half cent and one cent come from Nova Scotia, the bronze cent from Prince Edward Island, and the 1854 copper halfpenny and one penny, marked "currency," from New Brunswick. In 1843, New Brunswick had issued these same coins, but they were marked "token."

LATIN AMERICA

Most countries of Central and South America — or Latin America, as it is known — once belonged to the huge empire that the Spaniards conquered in the 16th century and ruled for 300 years. It stretched from Mexico in the north, down to Argentina and Chile at the southern tip of South America. The Spanish empire also included the island of Cuba and the Dominican Republic, which occupies half the island of Hispaniola. The only exceptions were French Guiana, British Guiana (now Guyana), Dutch Guiana (now Suriname), and Brazil, which was ruled by the Portuguese.

SPANISH NAMES

When these countries gained their freedom from Spain and Portugal, they kept the languages of their former rulers. This is why some of their coins and notes have Spanish names. Spain's currency comes in pesetas and centimos; in Latin America, Mexico, Colombia, Cuba, and Bolivia all use money valued in pesos and centavos.

This 25-centavo coin from Guatemala depicts the quetzal bird, the country's symbol.

MEXICO

The first coins of Latin America were struck in Mexico City in 1536, where the first mint in America had been opened a year earlier. Like other mints in the Spanish Empire, at Lima in Peru or Potosí in Bolivia, for example, the Mexico City mint produced large quantities of gold and silver coins. For a long time the coins, called "cobs," were rough and irregular. They were struck on pieces of metal sliced off bars that had not been rolled evenly. Their Spanish name was *cabo de barra*, or "cut from a bar," and that is just what they looked like.

These two irregular pieces of silver (right and below right) are "cobs" produced at the Mexico City mint some time between 1550 and 1610. From the conquests of Aztec Mexico and Inca Peru, the Spaniards acquired huge supplies of silver. It paid for Spain's expensive foreign wars.

Vasco Núñez de Balboa appears on this coin (bottom right) from Panama. Balboa was the first European to cross the Isthmus of Panama and see the Pacific Ocean. Panama, which did not become a separate country until 1903, gave its currency Balboa's name.

This 1837 Peruvian silver eight reales (above) was minted at Cuzco, capital of the old Inca empire, conquered by the Spanish in 1533.

This is a tiny note from Peru, issued in 1822 by José de San Martín, the liberator of Argentina, who also fought against the Spaniards in Peru and Chile.

PIECES OF EIGHT

In 1732 the Mexico mint received new and better machinery and started to produce the most famous coin in all of America: the Spanish eight reales, better known as the dollar. Later, the dollar became the chief currency of America; it was also used in the islands of the West Indies, in the Caribbean. Here, the dollar was often cut into pieces — the famous pieces of eight — and distributed to the islands.

The first country in Latin America to issue coins, Mexico was also the first to issue banknotes. In 1822, shortly after winning independence from Spain, the Mexicans printed one-peso and two-peso notes. Since then, Mexico has issued more banknotes than most other Latin American countries.

Mexican banknotes (right). The top one was issued by the state of Chihuahua during the revolution of 1910–1916, and the middle one by the state of Yucatán. The bottom note depicts an Aztec calendar stone.

COIN ALPHABETS

The alphabet used in this book, the Latin alphabet, is only one of several in the world today. And, of course, it is only one of many to appear on coins and banknotes. There are separate Greek, Russian, Thai, Hindi (Indian), and Arabic alphabets, all of them different from the Latin. There are also countries that use the Latin alphabet but call themselves by names different from those we know. For instance, the Swiss call their country "Helvetia" while we call it Switzerland. Spain is called "España" by Spaniards. Hungary is "Magyarország" to the Hungarians.

SOLVING THE PUZZLE

All these alphabets can cause problems when it comes to working out which country issued a coin or banknote. The pictures on these pages provide some hints on solving the problem. Or you could try a more painstaking method, such as going through a coin catalog and making a list of all countries that put different names on their coins.

If you do not like making long lists, show your "mysterious" coin to a collector or dealer, who can tell you where it comes from. Then write the information in a notebook so that if you come across another coin from the same country, you will know what it is.

In 1983, Thailand celebrated the 700th anniversary of the Thai alphabet with three commemorative coins. This is the lowest value, 10 baht. The obverse shows Buddha, who began Buddhism, the Thai religion. In the background is a Buddhist temple. The alphabet appears on the reverse.

NON-LATIN ALPHABETS

Coins inscribed with non-Latin alphabets are a bit more difficult to identify. Take, for instance, the Muslim countries, which follow the Islamic religion. Many of these countries use the Arabic alphabet. They do not put images on their coins, because image-making is forbidden by the Koran, the holy book of Islam. Instead, they use patterns and letters.

The best way to identify coins with non-Latin alphabets is to get photocopies of one or two coins from each of the countries. Stick them into your notebook, and refer to them each time you need to identify a coin. All this may seem complicated and tedious. However, when you have compared many coins with your notes, you will be able to recognize where they come from just by looking at them.

SOME NON-LATIN ALPHABETS

Europe	Bulgaria; Greece; states of the former Yugoslavia; states of the former USSR, such as the Ukraine.
Africa	Algeria,* Egypt,* Ethiopia, Libya,* Morocco,* Sudan,* Tunisia.*
Asia	Afghanistan,* Bangladesh, Burma, Cambodia, China, India, Japan, Korea, Laos, Nepal, Pakistan,* Sri Lanka, Taiwan, Thailand, Vietnam.
Middle East	Iran,* Iraq,* Israel, Saudi Arabia,* Syria.*
	* indicates a Muslim country

ALPHABETS OF THE WORLD

αβßγδεζηθικλμνξπορσςτυφφχψω
ΑΒΓΔΕΖΗΘΙΚΛΜΝΞΠΟΡΣΤΥΦΧ
ΨΩ 1234567890 .,:;!?

Οἱ πρῶτες ἐκδώσεις ἑλληνικῶν κειμένων ἔγιναν στό τυπο
είο τοῦ Ἄλδου Μανουτίου στή Βενετία. Ἀπό τό 1494 ὡς τό

Greek

абвгдежзийклмнопрстуфхцчшщъыьэ
юя АБВГДЕЖЗИЙКЛМНОПРСТУФХ
ЦЧШШЩЪЬЫЭЮЯ 1234567890 .,:;!?

Азот является одним из главных элементов входящих в состав ве
ществ, сбразующих живое тело растений и животных. В процесса

Cyrillic

ابتثتجحخدذرزسشصضطظعغفقكلمنهوىلا
١٢٣٤٥٦٧٨٩٠

فجهاز.السي ار ترونيك ٢٠٠ لايعتمد فى تصويره لاشكال
الحروف ، على عدسات أو مرايا أو قطع ميكانيكية متحركة

Arabic

किसी जाति के जीवन में उसके द्वारा प्रयुक्त शब्दों
का अत्यंत महत्त्वपूर्ण स्थान है । आवश्यकता तथा
स्थिति के अनुसार इन प्रयुक्त शब्दों का आगम

Indian

These coins are from Syria, Jordan, Iran, and Morocco. All are Muslim countries and use the Arabic alphabet.

Syria

Jordan

Morocco

Iran

The letters "CCCP" show that the coin on the right comes from the former USSR, which used the Cyrillic alphabet. In Cyrillic "C" reads as "S" and "P" as "R." So "CCCP" reads "SSSR" ("Union of Soviet Socialist Republics"). Bulgaria and the former Yugoslav states also use the Cyrillic alphabet.

The Israeli coin (below) uses the Hebrew, Arabic, and Latin alphabets. The coin from Ethiopia (bottom) uses the Amharic script, a modern form of an ancient Ethiopian writing used on coins by the 4th century A.D.

An easy way to identify coins of Greece (above left) is to look for the "E" and two upside-down "V"s. In the Greek alphabet this spells "ELL," the first letters of ELLAS, the Greek name for Greece.

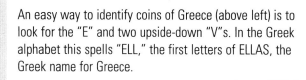

These banknotes (left) come from Japan. As you can see, the Japanese characters are all separate.

ASIA

After coins were first introduced by Greek colonists in western Turkey, the idea of coinage spread eastward into Asia. It reached India in the early 4th century B.C. Later, Indian ideas about coin design influenced the coins of countries as far apart as Nepal in the Himalayas and Indonesia in Southeast Asia.

The gold denara (above left) from India was struck in about A.D. 350. The copper coin (above right) comes from 7th-century Nepal. Although the metals they are made from are different, these two coins are very similar.

INDIAN COINS

India's first coins, found by archaeologists in the north of the country, were small dish-shaped pieces of silver stamped or punch-marked on one side. Later, many empires were established in India; they issued their own coins. The last to be formed, after 1526, was the Mogul Empire. The Moguls were Muslims, so their coins often carried Arabic inscriptions and verses of Arabic poetry.

UNUSUAL SHAPES

However, India was not the first Asian country to have coins. The Chinese used them 200 years earlier, in the 6th century B.C. It seems that the Chinese invented coins quite separately from the Greeks in Turkey. The first coins were in the form of metal knives, cowrie shells, or hoes, and many later Chinese coins had square holes in the center, with lettering around them.

From China, coins soon spread to countries such as Korea, Vietnam, and Japan. In the 13th century, many Chinese coins circulated in Japan. At this time, the Chinese had begun using banknotes, so they exported, or sent, to Japan the coins they did not need.

Modern Asian coins look like European or American coins. This silver dollar from China was minted in 1912.

It is easy to see where the Koreans got their ideas about coin design. The Korean bronze coin (left) was struck in 1423. It looks very much like the Chinese bronze coin of 1408 (below).

This is a silver bar coin from 18th-century Laos (left). It is punch-marked with a boat, an elephant, and a chakra, or petal, design, just as early Indian coins were.

Banknotes from Kampuchea (Cambodia) are common in job lots. Many show subjects such as agriculture, industry, and fishing (below) in their beautiful traditional patterned borders. However, a recent 500-riel note pictured a battle. Kampuchea, with Vietnam and Laos, lies in the area once known as Indochina, where wars have been fought for over 50 years.

A CHECKERED HISTORY

The region we call the Middle East is really the western part of Asia. The coins of this area show how often different conquerors have ruled it. In the ancient past, Syria, Lebanon, and Jordan used Greek-type coins. Later, when this area was conquered by the Romans, Roman coins were used. Then, when Muslims ruled there, Arabic-type coins were used, many of them covered in inscriptions.

After 1096, when the Christian Crusaders conquered kingdoms in what are now Israel, Jordan, and Lebanon, another type of coinage came to the Middle East. At first, these coins were like the Islamic coins of Egypt, until the pope protested and made the Crusaders put a cross and other Christian symbols on their currency.

THE MIDDLE EAST

Before the discovery of routes around Africa, trade between Europe and Asia passed through the Middle East. The coinage of the region reflects the many nations that have ruled and traded there.

A Roman silver coin from Syria, showing the emperor Caracalla (A.D. 188–217).

A 12th-century Crusader gold bezant from the Holy Land (Israel).

A silver drachm of the emperor Trajan showing a camel from Roman Jordan.

A copper fals minted by the Muslim caliphs of the Umayyad dynasty who ruled in Lebanon in the 8th century A.D.

NOT ALL COINS ARE ROUND

Modern India has often used non-round coins. Here are a scallop-edged 10 paise of 1971, one anna of 1915, and two paise of 1972. The two paise bears the lions emblem of the national coat of arms.

When you think of a coin, you usually think of something round. This is a convenient shape which is easy to handle. Not all coins are round, though. Many have other, more interesting shapes. Some are very attractive, like the petal-shaped eight-anna coins of Burma, struck in 1949, the diamond-shaped two annas of India (1950), and the 12-sided five cents of Canada (1943).

FAME AND FORTUNE

A famous and rare coin, the $50 gold piece issued by the USA in 1915 for the Panama Pacific Exposition, is octagonal (eight sides). Its design was taken directly from the coins of ancient Athens: The goddess Athena appears on the obverse and the owl on the reverse.

In 1919, the Straits Settlements (former British Colonies in Southeast Asia) struck square one-cent coins. Like other coins with corners or angles, these had rounded corners so that there would be no sharp edges to scratch the hand or tear holes in pockets and purses.

These six coins below are a Jamaican cent, a 20 cents from Swaziland, a 10 shillings of Guernsey, a 25 cents of Malta, a five centimos of the Philippines, and a 10 pesos from Mexico.

In 1969 Australia replaced its circular silver 50 cents with a dodecagonal (12-sided) cupronickel 50 cents (above left). It bears the Australian coat of arms. The Canadian 50 cents appears to have 12 sides, too, but is in fact round. The British threepenny coin was less popular with collectors than the round silver coin it replaced.

52

UNPOPULAR DESIGNS

Despite their apparent attractiveness, coins that are not round have sometimes been unpopular. One of these was the thick and chunky dodecagonal, or 12-sided, "threepenny bit" of Great Britain, first struck in 1937. This replaced the small, slimmer silver threepenny bit which was, and still is, a favorite coin among collectors. There was also a big fuss after 1969, when the large seven-sided 50-pence piece was first struck in Britain as one of the new decimal coins.

In 1975–1976 Hong Kong introduced these three non-round coins: a scallop-edged 20 cents and two dollars, and a 10-sided five dollars.

ROUND OR NOT ROUND?

Why do many people dislike coins that are not round? Most coins are round and people are used to them being that shape. And they usually like what they are used to. Even so, coins that are not round do have one big advantage: whether you are collecting them or doing your shopping with them, their different shape makes them easy to see among other coins. This can be important in a country that uses a lot of coins, where people might have a great deal of small change in their purses or pockets. It also means that people who do not have strong eyesight can more easily feel what sort of coin they are holding.

This looks more like a wax seal than a coin. It is a silver bracteate denar struck in 13th-century Switzerland.

This is a really strange non-round coin, issued in Ireland in 1642. Its rough appearance shows that it was emergency money for use during a civil war. It was called Inchiquin money and was made from lumps of metal stamped with their weight.

Here is a coin to fool you! This 50 escudos of Portugal (right) shows an ocean-going ship, a symbol of Portugal's sea-faring tradition. It looks as if it has nine sides but is in fact round. Only the inner rim of the coin has nine sides.

Like the Irish coin above, this silver one from the Netherlands was emergency money. It was struck in the city of Leiden in 1574. The coin die was obviously round, but it was struck on a diamond-shaped piece of silver.

AFRICA

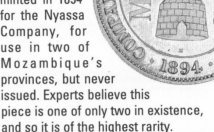
Coins came very slowly to Africa, even though the Greek settlements in Libya, in the north, were using silver staters and small coins called fractions in the late 6th century B.C. That was only 50 years or so after they had first appeared in western Turkey. Later, coins spread to Roman colonies in North Africa and to Carthage, a city founded by Phoenicians from Syria and situated near modern Tunis.

In 1882 the sultan of Zanzibar, an independent island, issued a new coinage inscribed in Arabic. This coin is a very rare silver half ryal. Previously, Zanzibar had used coins from the Islamic Middle East and China.

This is a 15th-century base silver coin from Mogadishu. Now the capital city of modern Somalia, Mogadishu was ruled by a Muslim sultan. This is why the coin has Arabic inscriptions.

GOING WITH THE TRADE

At this time, some 2,500 years ago, coins went where merchants and traders went. The first coins known in Ethiopia, for instance, were taken there about A.D. 50 by traders who used Roman coins to buy goods. In the same way, in the 11th century A.D., coins were introduced into Kenya by Arab traders who came to buy ivory and slaves.

If you find out when African countries first had coins, you will see that those bordering the sea had coins long before others inland. This was largely because early traders in Africa were not usually explorers, and Africa was a huge, dangerous, and mysterious continent. It was much easier and safer to trade with people who lived by the sea.

This is an early silver coin from Libya, the first place in Africa to have coins. The coin is very Greek, though. Its denomination, four drachmas, is Greek. It shows the head of Zeus, ruler of the Greek gods, and there is Greek lettering on it. The coin was struck in about 470 B.C.

AFRICA

In 1968, Sudan issued this cupronickel 25-ghirsh coin (below) showing a mailman delivering letters by camel.

Until 1975, Angola had been part of the Portuguese empire for nearly 500 years. This copper 40-reis coin of King Joseph of Portugal (above) was struck in 1757.

EUROPEAN EMPIRES

Many centuries passed before European explorers and missionaries began to travel inland. Eventually, most of Africa came to be divided among the Portuguese, the British, French, Germans, Spanish, Belgians, and Italians. Naturally, they brought their coins and currency with them.

Rule by Europeans has now ended. The last of the larger colonies, Portuguese Mozambique and Angola, gained their independence in 1975. However, many independent African countries still use European coinage. The French franc, for example, is the currency in former French colonies such as Niger, Chad, Burkina Faso, and Cameroon. The British shilling is used in Kenya, Uganda, and Somalia, and in Tanzania, where it is called "shilingi."

BRITISH AND FRENCH COLONIAL COINS

These four coins come from countries in the French and British empires in Africa. If you compare them with French and British coins it should be possible to decide from which empire they came.

A three-penny coin of Nigeria (British).

An East African 50 cents/half shilling (British).

A 100 francs of Cameroon (French).

A franc of Madagascar (French).

These banknotes are a five shillings from Biafra, independent from Nigeria from 1967 to 1970; a 20 francs from the Belgian Congo (now Zaire, Rwanda, and Burundi); a Sudanese 10 pounds, withdrawn from use when the president pictured was deposed; and a one pound from Rhodesia (now Zimbabwe), with a watermark of Rhodesia's founder, Cecil Rhodes.

AUSTRALIA AND OCEANIA

The islands of the Pacific Ocean (Oceania) have a varied history, and this is reflected in their money. For example, the Mariana Islands were visited by a Portuguese explorer in 1521. The Spanish controlled the islands until the largest island, Guam, was taken over by the U.S. in 1899. The others were passed to Germany. From 1941 until 1945 they were occupied by Japan, and now are administered by the U.S. So Spanish, German, Japanese, and U.S. currency have all been used there.

EARLY EUROPEAN EXPLORATION

The Pacific islands, together with Australia and New Zealand, have had their own coins for less than 200 years. The first coins made for use in this vast area, which covers one-third of the earth's surface, were not produced until 1813.

Why were coins so late in reaching this part of the world? The reason is that this was the last great region of the globe to be visited by European explorers, such as France's Louis-Antoine de Bougainville and the Netherlands' Abel Tasman. The Pacific Ocean was first crossed by a Spanish fleet in 1521, and traders such as the Dutch set up island trading posts. The Pacific was not thoroughly explored and mapped, though, until James Cook made three voyages covering the ocean between 1768 and 1779. One of Cook's landings was on the eastern coast of Australia. In 1788 the British set up a colony there, at Sydney.

AUSTRALIA'S FIRST COINS

The colonists were mostly convicts transported, or sent away, from Britain as punishment for crimes. Neither they nor the aboriginal ("native") peoples had coins, so they used barter instead. They bartered food and drink, especially rum. They also used Dutch, Portuguese, Spanish, and Indian coins that they received through trade. Most of these foreign coins were used to buy food and goods from other foreign traders; soon there was a shortage of small change.

The reverses of these Australian bronze one-penny and half-penny coins show a great red kangaroo, Australia's symbol. The other half-penny has an earlier design, and was struck between 1911 and 1936.

Two coins in one. The "holey dollar" was originally a Spanish silver dollar. The central "plug," when punched out, was worth one shilling and threepence. The outer ring was worth five shillings, four times as much.

This 1967 French Polynesian 50 francs shows one of the islands, with outrigger canoes, huts, and coconut palms.

New Guinea, now part of Papua New Guinea, was a German colony when this silver two-mark coin was struck in 1894. Its reverse shows one of the islands' birds of paradise.

HOLEY DOLLARS

At last, it was decided that Australia must have its own coins. The first were the "holey dollars" of New South Wales, in eastern Australia. Holey dollars were made by punching out a small "plug" worth a fifth of the whole coin from the centers of 40,000 Spanish silver dollars. Then, in 1824, £100,000 of British coins were brought into Australia. Other people, usually traders, issued tokens, mostly copper or bronze pennies and halfpennies. Real coins were not struck in Australia until 1855, when a mint was set up in Sydney following the discovery of gold in Australia four years earlier. Later, New Zealand and other British colonies in the Pacific, such as the Solomon Islands, Fiji, and Tonga, used British, Australian, and other coins until they acquired their own.

TOO BIG FOR A POCKET

The Caroline Islands, a U.S. territory, have had a variety of coins. However, the islanders have preferred to use their own forms of money. On one of the islands, called Yap, this money was in the form of huge stones, used in special ceremonies.

This 1969 New Zealand dollar (above left) shows the first complete map of the islands, drawn by Captain Cook (left), and the *Endeavour*, one of his ships (right). New Zealand's first coin was a silver threepence (above right) issued in 1933. Until then, New Zealanders had used Australian and British coins.

FINDING TREASURE

People often hope to find treasure trove — rare and valuable historical objects — by chance. Treasure *has* been discovered in this way but, sadly, not as often as people like to think. In order to make a great find, you usually have to work for it, either by diving for buried treasure in the sea or by digging for it on land.

UNDER THE SEA

Some of the most famous coin finds have been made in shipwrecks. The invention of the Aqua-Lung (air tanks and a mask) in 1943 by the French naval officer Jacques Cousteau has allowed archaeologists to work deep underwater.

Unfortunately, treasure seekers have used the Aqua-Lung to find and loot these wrecks. By the end of the 1950s, every known wreck off the South of France had been destroyed, and hundreds were looted in the Caribbean and off Florida.

WINDOWS INTO THE PAST

If they are studied carefully, shipwrecks and other archaeological sites can tell us a great deal about our history. Treasure seekers who loot and damage these sites are destroying valuable windows into our past. Often they are trespassing on private property and breaking the law. If you think you have found a treasure hoard or a historical site — coins, pottery, or any other historical items — report your discovery to the police and your local archaeological club.

SOLVING THE PUZZLE

Finding coins has often helped archaeologists in their studies of historical sites. In 1973 the remains of a 115-foot Chinese trading ship were found near the port of Quanzhou. Among the items found with the ship were over 500 brass coins, the most recent dating from 1265 to 1274. More remarkable still, scientists studying the way the ship had been built found seven bronze coins hidden in the keel. The coins were arranged to represent the constellation Ursa Major (also known as the Great Bear or Plow). The coins were probably put there to bring good luck to the ship. By studying the coins, details of which are known to collectors, it has been possible to date the ship to about 1277.

These pieces of eight are typical of the coins used by Dutch merchants in the Far East in the 17th and 18th centuries. The Dutch East India Company was one of the world's leading trading companies. As its ships sailed the Indian and Pacific oceans, some were lost in storms. Among the lost were the *Vergulde Draeck*, carrying 10,000 coins, and the *Zuytdorp*, from which divers recovered over 7,000 coins in just a few hours.

SUTTON HOO

In about A.D. 625 an Anglo-Saxon king was buried with his ship at Sutton Hoo in Britain. Among the magnificent treasure were Merovingian tremisses, from Frankia (France). These gold coins had been minted at the 37 different sites shown on the map. This find indicates the importance of coins, and therefore trade, in Frankia.

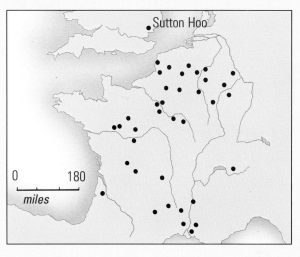

WRECKED IN STORMS

Some of the biggest coin finds have come from 16th- and 17th-century Spanish ships. After discovering the Americas, Spain ruthlessly exploited the riches of the "New World." Between 1500 and 1660, over 15,000 tons of silver were shipped to Spain. The Spanish vessels soon became targets for pirates and privateers (private ships licensed by governments to capture the enemy's merchant ships), and were forced to sail together for protection.

These heavily armed treasure fleets had little defense against the weather, however. In 1715 a hurricane wrecked 10 ships of a convoy. Worse was to follow, for in 1733 at least 16 ships were lost in a storm off the Florida Keys. Thousands of people were drowned, and huge quantities of coins and other treasure went to the bottom of the sea. Archaeologists are still finding and studying wrecks such as these.

These pieces of two, four, and eight reales (right) were recovered from Spanish galleons wrecked in the Americas in the 17th and 18th centuries. In 1554 three ships were shipwrecked off southern Texas. Some silver coins and other treasure were removed from the wrecks by a private treasure-hunting company. Scientists were outraged because the site had not been mapped and the find recorded. The company was forced to hand over the treasure so archaeologists could study it.

A RICH TREASURE

In the spring of 1840, some workmen were repairing the walls by the banks of the Ribble River, near Preston in northwest England, when one of them looked more closely at the pile of mud the gang had dug up. He saw some gray, muddy disks. When he removed the dirt from one of the disks, he realized it was a silver coin. What is more, there were thousands of them, as the workmen soon discovered.

When they had finished, they had unearthed silver objects and 8,000 coins from the days of King Alfred the Great, a thousand years before. This great find was called the Cuerdale Hoard.

These are coins and objects from the Cuerdale Hoard. At first no one knew who had buried them. Then scholars discovered that, in A.D. 911, a Danish army in the midst of raiding northern England was attacked by the English. The Danes fled, but it seems they buried their treasure first. They never recovered it.

WAITING TO BE FOUND

Not all coin finds have been as easy as this, but there are surely many great coin hoards that have not yet been discovered. Treasure was often buried in times of war or revolution. Much of it has never been reclaimed. At sea, the waters are still full of ships that sank hundreds of years ago, just like those in the Caribbean or along the Florida Keys. It may be difficult or dangerous to recover lost hoards from these ships, but there are always treasure seekers who will try.

On land, archaeologists probably have the best opportunities of finding coins. In fact, it is their job to dig up treasure and other objects from the past. Many finds are made when investigating sites where roads and buildings are being constructed.

This 15th-century manuscript shows a peasant finding a hoard of buried coins. At this time, treasure seekers tried magic spells to help them find hoards.

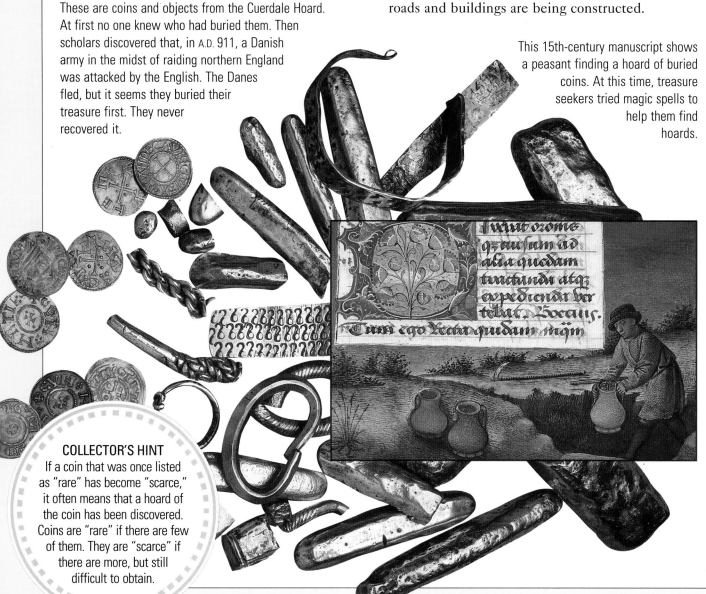

COLLECTOR'S HINT
If a coin that was once listed as "rare" has become "scarce," it often means that a hoard of the coin has been discovered. Coins are "rare" if there are few of them. They are "scarce" if there are more, but still difficult to obtain.

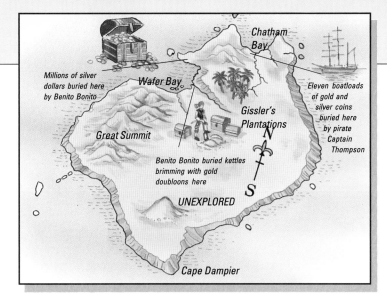

Millions of silver dollars buried here by Benito Bonito

Wafer Bay

Chatham Bay

Great Summit

Gissler's Plantations

Benito Bonito buried kettles brimming with gold doubloons here

Eleven boatloads of gold and silver coins buried here by pirate Captain Thompson

UNEXPLORED

Cape Dampier

This map of Cocos Island in the Pacific Ocean was made about a century ago. It shows where the Portuguese pirate Benito Bonito buried two hoards of coins in about 1820. The map also says that another pirate, Captain Thompson, buried treasure in the north of the island. Treasure seekers are still looking for these hoards!

MUD AND METAL

There are many people who use metal detectors to search for coins and metal objects. These metal detectives are like amateur archaeologists. They go metal detecting for fun and excitement as well as for the chance of finding objects of value.

Mudlarkers are like metal detectives, but search the mud along the banks of rivers hoping to find old coins and other objects long buried in the mud or washed up there by the river. In the past, mudlarkers were often young boys who searched for anything of interest that they could exchange for food and clothing.

THE RIGHT PLACE

Mudlarkers and metal detectives have to know where they have the best chance of finding treasure. They know, for example, that the Romans used to throw coins into rivers as gifts to the river gods, and where there were Roman or other settlements long ago.

Today's mudlarkers are often adults, and they need a special license or permission to search. The metal detectives, too, need permission from the owners of the land they search. Otherwise, they could be arrested for trespassing. Never go mudlarking, because rivers can be dangerous places. Nevertheless, always keep an eye out when walking along the seashore, or digging in the garden — who knows what treasure you might find?

TREASURE TROVE

In many countries there is a law of "treasure trove." Under such a law, any treasure that is found automatically belongs to the whole country, not to the finder. If the treasure is considered to be of significant historical or artistic value, the finder is usually given a reward or compensation. Less important treasure is often returned to the finder. There is no law of treasure trove in the U.S., and people are allowed to keep their find if it is genuinely believed to have no owner.

A metal detector is an instrument for discovering metal objects, such as coins, below the surface of the ground. When metal is detected, a signal sounds in the headphones, or a light flashes. Coin dealers often go metal detecting and sell their finds at the markets where they trade.

MISTAKES AND FORGERIES

There are not many mistakes on coins. However, the ones that do exist are not necessarily very valuable, because coin collectors do not seem to think that all mistakes are important. (They are unlike stamp collectors, for whom collecting mistakes, printing errors, and marks is an important part of the hobby.) This means you can probably buy some of these coin errors at a reasonable price, and they will make an interesting addition to your collection.

SIMPLE ERRORS

Some mistakes are very small. A figure on a date may be upside down, or a period could be missing. For example, the *"gratia"* in the *"dei gratia"* (Latin for "By the Grace of God") on a British coin of 1690 reads *"gretia"* instead. Sometimes a date will get mixed up. Some British five-shilling coins of King William III struck in 1696 have the date 1669 instead — 20 years before William became king!

This is a $10 gold coin issued by Canada for the 1976 Olympic Games. Unfortunately, on some of the coins "1974" was put in place of the correct date, 1976. These coins are rare and worth nearly 40 times more than this "1976" coin.

FREAKS

Freaks are coins that are badly made or misstruck. Some occur because coins "jump" when they are struck, and this can affect the milling around the edge (see page 29). Half the graining may not be there, leaving the edge smooth and plain. You may find other freaks with no top surface. This is caused by an air bubble getting into the bar from which the blanks are cut. Sometimes the bubble will cause the coin to break in two when it is dropped on its edge. Usually, freaks are discovered and discarded by examiners at the mint. Any freaks you find have somehow been missed and slipped into circulation.

The obverse of a coin is meant to have a different design from the reverse. This coin (right) is a freak. It has the same design on both sides. This happens when a coin fails to fall from the striking machine after it has been struck. The blank for making the next coin comes between the die and the first coin. When the striking machine next operates, the coin already struck impresses its design onto one side of the blank.

On the coin on the right, the area around the head of the trident (right) has been damaged by an object getting between the metal blank and the die.

FORGERIES

Forgeries are much more serious than freaks because they are false coins or notes. At one time, forgers were executed and their bodies left in public places as a warning to others. This did not stop the forgers.

Many forgeries of ancient Greek and Roman coins have been made, and gold coins from the U.S. have been copied. Many banknotes issued during Latin American wars have been extensively counterfeited (illegally copied), as have banknotes of the Ottoman Empire (Turkey) and New Zealand £5 notes, both in the 19th century. Also in the 19th century, many forgeries were made of the Ming notes of China printed 500 years earlier.

Banknotes have been forged during wartime to damage an enemy's economy or for propaganda. The white five-pound note below is a very accurate German World War II copy of a real note, and has only slight mistakes in the design. The Japanese note was forged by American forces in 1943–1944. It is a propaganda forgery. On the back, in Japanese, it urges Japanese soldiers to surrender.

FORGED OR GENUINE?

With modern coins, it can be very difficult to tell a forgery from the real thing, but forgeries of older coins are easier to detect. These forgeries do not always weigh the same as the genuine coins. Find out the correct weight from a dealer or expert, then check your coin and see if it weighs the same.

The coin on the left has been forged by plating a copper disk with silver. The copper can be seen showing through the worn plating.

This Mexican dollar is a Chinese forgery made by putting a thin silver case around a disk of tin.

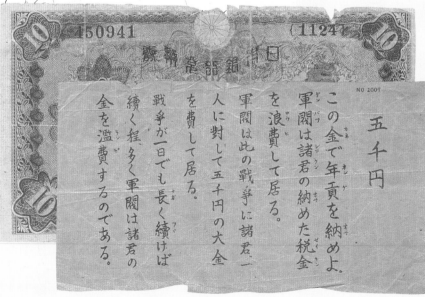

The real purpose of this very good "forgery" of an English guinea (21 shillings) would be found on the reverse. Made in brass in the 18th century, it was in fact an imitation created for advertising purposes.

STRANGE AND FAMOUS

Some coins become famous because of their size, others because of the images they carry. A record price of $900,000 was paid in the 1970s for a $20 gold pattern because it was the only one known to be in existence. Whatever makes a coin famous, though, they all have one thing in common: They are unusual in some way and so are different from the millions of other coins that have been struck.

THE FIRST PORTRAIT

Of course, the coin that carried the first portrait of a living person is famous. Before the silver tetradrachm, struck in Egypt between 323 and 305 B.C., coins most often showed ancient gods and goddesses. This tetradrachm carried the portrait of Ptolemy I, one of Alexander the Great's generals, who founded a new kingdom in Egypt in 323 B.C. Another portrait which makes a coin famous is the picture of the Man in the Moon which appears on the reverse of a silver thaler of 1547 struck in Lüneburg, Germany.

The "Man in the Moon" coin of 1547 came from Lüneburg in Germany. The name of the city was like the Latin word for moon: *luna*.

LARGE AND HEAVY

A 100-ducat coin struck in Hungary in 1629 is well known for being the largest gold coin ever produced. Two other coins famous for their size and also their weight were the penny and two-penny "Cartwheels" issued in Britain in 1797. They got their nickname because they were very thick and had a raised rim around the edge, just like the wheel of a cart.

The famous "Cartwheel" penny and two-penny coins were struck in Britain only in 1797. The tiny coin is a 1937 Maundy one-penny, from a special set of coins issued by the monarch to poor people each year.

PATTERNS AND PROOFS

These two gold Greek coins are extremely rare. The one on the left is a pattern from the reign of King Paul (1947–1964). Patterns are produced as experiments before the final coins are minted for issue. The pattern has to be approved by the royal family or head of state before the coins can be minted. This coin is special because it is one of four coins in the only set of its kind known to be in private hands and offered for sale. Usually, gold patterns are given to the royal family or national museums. They are not listed in catalogs. The coin on the right shows a proof 30 drachmas of the reign of King Constantine II (1964–1967). It is extremely rare because it was specially struck in gold after the normal currency issue had been minted in silver.

This is a famous and frightening banknote. In 1954, the Canadian Central Bank issued a series of banknotes showing Queen Elizabeth II (right). Unfortunately, the curls in the queen's hair were drawn so that the face of a devil appeared (below right). Many people refused to use the notes and eventually they were taken out of circulation and replaced.

INFLATION

Other strange and famous coins and banknotes are evidence of wars and emergencies. Inflation, for example, occurs when money loses its value, and enormous amounts of it are needed to buy the most ordinary things, like a loaf of bread or a newspaper. Very serious inflation occurred in Germany in the 1920s and in Hungary in the late 1940s. As a result, one famous German note of 1923 had a value of one billion marks. In 1945 and 1946, banknotes issued in Hungary had values of up to one billion pengö. At about the same time in Greece, notes for 500 million drachmas were being issued.

This German 100-million-mark note (left) was issued in November 1923, during a time of hyperinflation. It was worth less than five dollars in today's money.

THE FUTURE OF CURRENCY

In a well-known science fiction film, called *Star Trek IV: The Voyage Home*, Captain Kirk and his crew travel 300 years back in time to the late 20th century. Kirk finds that coins and banknotes are still being used. To get some, he has to sell an antique pair of spectacles. In Kirk's own time, the 23rd century, no one uses money any more. Instead, they have "credits" and their "money" exists only in computer records.

OTHER MONEY

There have always been other forms of money, even in the hundreds of years that coins and banknotes have existed, though completely computerized money has not yet been introduced. The nearest we have gotten so far is "money of account," which is a currency used only by accountants when making financial records. The ECU (European Currency Unit) used in the European Community is money of account. In the European Monetary System, the currency of each member country is given a value in ECUs so that the rate of exchange between them is stabilized, or kept properly balanced.

COMPUTERIZED MONEY

We are approaching computerized money with credit and account cards, automatic teller cards, and telephone cards. These have been called "plastic" money because the cards are made of plastic. People can also do their shopping by a plastic card method in which the amount spent is debited, or charged, directly to their bank account by computer.

Below is an unofficial proof set of British ECU coins, issued by a private mint. Plastic money includes credit and check guarantee cards (below left), which can also be used to get money from an automatic teller machine (ATM), and ATM cards (below, with the black stripe), which can be used only at an ATM. With a credit card, you have to pay only part of the total due at the end of the month. With a store charge card, you have to pay all of it.

Other forms of money such as checks, banker's drafts, postal or bank money orders, and promissory notes use paper. With these, banks — or in the case of postal orders, the post office — are instructed to transfer money from one person to another. As it happens, banknotes are also promissory notes, even though people think of them as real money. You can see this if you read what some banknotes say. A £5 British banknote, for example, says: "The Bank of England promise to pay the bearer the sum of five pounds."

Promissory notes (the one top right was written in 1730 and begins "Pray pay . . ."), checks (right and below right), travelers' checks, and pay warrants (bottom) are not money, but they represent it. Checks are used most often. They are much safer than money, because they are payable only to the person or company whose name appears after "Pay to the order of."

Telephone cards (left) have many interesting designs and are very collectable. The painter Vincent van Gogh, an elephant, and a cartoon chicken are on three cards shown here. The train is on a Japanese card used to pay for railroad tickets.

People buy postal orders (below left) at post offices and bank money orders at banks. Unlike checks, postal and bank money orders do not have to be signed by the person sending them. The person who receives one signs and hands it over at the post office or bank to be paid in cash.

TOKENS

Tokens are substitute money, used instead of coins. They are not forged or false, though. As long as they are exchanged for the value shown on them, people are willing to accept them as if they were real money. It can be fascinating to collect tokens, many of which have remarkable stories behind them.

IN TIME OF WAR

Often, tokens are produced and used when there is a shortage of real coins. For example, when a town was besieged, the inhabitants might hoard or save real coins. In 1574, in Leiden in the Netherlands, leather book bindings were cut up, stamped, and used instead of money.

Many tokens were issued during World War I. In Germany, bronze coins were melted down to make war goods, and rising prices forced the silver ones out of circulation. The shortage was not eased by issuing aluminum, zinc, and iron coins, so tokens were issued. Called *Notmünzen*, they were no more successful than the cheap metal coins, and so emergency notes called *Notgelden* (see page 19) were printed in amazing quantities.

This ivory token was used on private plantations in the Keeling (Cocos) Islands

CIVIL WAR

Token coins were also struck in times of civil war, as in England in the mid-17th century or the USA between 1861 and 1865. The American Civil War practice of issuing tokens consisting of postage stamps stuck to metal discs was copied during World War I. During the civil war that followed the Russian Revolution in 1917, the postage stamps were printed on thick card and used as money tokens.

A SHORTAGE OF COINS

At other times, tokens were issued because there were not enough real coins in the low values that people used for change. In Great Britain, the government failed to issue any copper coins for over 20 years, between 1775 and 1797. So businesses issued halfpenny and

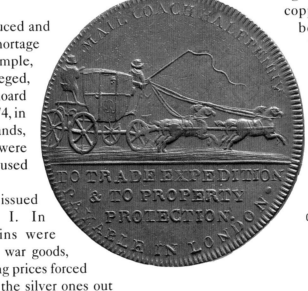

This British halfpenny mail-coach token shows a coach and horses with the driver holding the reins. It was issued for John Palmer "in gratitude for benefits received from the establishment of mail coaches." Palmer had introduced the mail coaches in 1784.

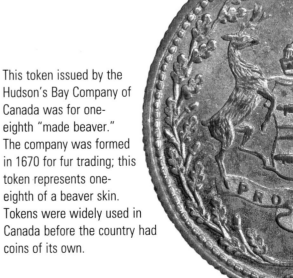

This token issued by the Hudson's Bay Company of Canada was for one-eighth "made beaver." The company was formed in 1670 for fur trading; this token represents one-eighth of a beaver skin. Tokens were widely used in Canada before the country had coins of its own.

penny tokens instead. One British mining company on the Welsh island of Anglesey made tokens from local copper with a portrait of a druid, a priest of the ancient pagan religion, on the obverse, and these were soon being used in other parts of the country. Other tradesmen and companies copied these tokens and, before long, many thousands of them were in circulation. Some very beautiful tokens were specially made to appeal to collectors.

ADVERTISING TOKENS

Other tokens, called tradesmen's tokens, are meant for advertising the services or goods offered by the shopkeepers or manufacturers who produce them. In the 19th century, tokens produced by public institutions, such as workhouses, were exchanged for food, shelter, or clothes. Tokens issued by factory and mine owners had to be exchanged by their workers in the canteens where they ate their meals.

This salung token of about 1850 was made in porcelain, for use in a gambling house in Thailand. Gambling houses all over the world have "chips" or tokens. Gamblers buy them to use for placing their bets at gambling tables.

What do you use for money in a place where money is made? This token, used at the Royal Mint, Llantrisant, Wales, has been made to be different from the coins struck there.

During an economic crisis in 1922–1923, the French chamber of commerce issued one-franc (left and below left), two-franc, and 50-centime tokens. They were inscribed "Bon Pour" ("Good For") and the value. The name is now often used for tokens — "bon-pours," or "good-fors," indicating the token's value.

This is a German 10-pfennig token issued in 1917, during World War I. Over 7,000 types of this war money were issued by over 1,000 cities, towns, and businesses.

COIN AND NOTE TERMS

Like most hobbies, coin and banknote collecting is a world of its own. Everyone talks using words and terms most people have never heard of before, or, if they have heard them, they are used in a different way: reverse, obverse, proof, die, strike, cast, uncirculated, and many more. Here's a selection of terms that you will come across when reading about coins and banknotes.

Ag. The chemical symbol for the metal silver. Other metals are described by the symbols **Al** (aluminum), **Au** (gold), **Cu** (copper), **Fe** (iron), **Mg** (magnesium), **Ni** (nickel), **Pt** (platinum), **Sn** (tin), and **Zn** (zinc). Brass (**Bra**) and bronze (**Br** or **Ae**) are alloys, mixtures of metals.

Banknote. Paper money issued by a bank controlled by a government. In many countries the holder of the note is guaranteed payment in coinage on request.

Banker's Note. Paper money issued by private banks and institutions.

Base Metal Commemorative. A commemorative coin made from a base (non-precious) metal rather than from a precious metal such as silver or gold.

Bills of Credit. An American term for Continental and Colonial paper-money issues.

Branch Bank Notes. Issues from different branches of the same bank. Each branch may have its own design, or just the name of its city on the note.

Card Money. Emergency issues of the late 18th and early 19th centuries in Canada and France. Because of a shortage of paper, the notes were made from playing cards.

Certificates. U.S. paper money in the form of a receipt for gold and silver.

Colonial Currency. Paper money of the American states when they were still British colonies.

Continental Currency. Paper money that circulated in North America between 1775 and 1779.

Currency. All money circulating at a particular time.

Cut Notes. Paper money cut into halves or quarters, usually during a shortage of coins. The halves or quarters may be overprinted with the new value of the note.

Decimal Currency. A system of money based on a unit divided into tenths or hundredths. For example, 100 Australian cents = one dollar. Before 1966, Australia had a non-decimal currency of 12 pence = one shilling; two shillings = one florin; 20 shillings = one pound.

Denomination. The name given to a coin or note — e.g., franc or dollar.

Difference Marks. Letters or symbols indicating that the purity and weight of the coin have been tested. Also known as sequence marks.

Encased Postage Stamps. Tokens made by attaching postage stamps to metal frames.

Fiduciary Issues. Banknotes circulated without the backing of gold or any other security.

Fineness. Proportion of precious metal (silver, gold, or platinum) contained in a coin.

Fractional Currency. Paper money with a denomination that is less than the standard unit — e.g., a U.S. 50-cent note, which is less than the standard U.S. dollar.

Good-fors. Emergency notes or tokens of low denomination.

Indented Note. Paper money with a shaped edge. The redeemed note would be matched with a stub kept by the issuing bank, so that counterfeit notes could be detected.

Inflation Notes. Notes of very high denomination issued by countries suffering from hyperinflation (very rapidly rising prices).

Invasion Money. Official money given to soldiers of the Allied military forces for use in Germany, Italy, Japan, and France during World War II. See also *Occupation Money*.

Mint Mark. A letter or symbol showing at which mint a coin was struck.

Notaphilist. A person who studies paper money.

Numismatics. The study of coins and medals.

Occupation Money. Military currency introduced to a country by the occupying army.

Overprints. Markings on a note to show that it has been canceled, revalued, etc. A note will be overprinted "specimen" if it is to be used for publicity purposes or it is sent to other organizations as a reference sample.

Patina. Crust (usually of dirt) on the surface of a coin. The green deposit often seen on brass or copper coins (right) is verdigris (vert = green), a coating of copper sulfate or carbonate. It will form on coins kept in damp conditions.

Pattern. A coin produced to test new designs and minting processes. Patterns are usually struck on carefully prepared blanks. "Trial pieces" are coins struck during the preparation of dies to check the progress of work, and might even be on irregular pieces of metal. Many patterns are never issued.

Piedfort. A coin struck with greater thickness, usually for presentation purposes.

Portrait. A likeness of a person or animal, used as a design on coins and banknotes. A double portrait has two persons on the same side of the coin. When the two people face each other, the design is "vis-à-vis" or *bajoire*. More commonly they are "jugate" or conjoined — that is, they face the same way, as shown on this coin.

Private Money. Money issued by organizations (e.g., shops) rather than that authorized by the government.

Privy Mark. These letters or symbols indicate the chief engraver of a coin, or the director of the mint. See also *Mint Mark*.

Promissory Notes. Documents that promise to pay on demand, or after a fixed period of time, a specific sum of money. All banknotes are promissory notes, because they promise to pay the bearer on demand the sum of money shown on the note.

Provenance Mark. Letters or symbols identifying the source of the metal from which a coin is made. The letters "SSC" on the coin on the right show that the coin's silver was supplied by the South Seas Company.

Rag Money. American term for paper money.

Raised Note. A note that has been overprinted to increase its denomination.

Reform (of currency). A complete change in the monetary system of a country.

Reissues. Issues that are recirculated after a break in circulation; they usually have an overprint.

Remainders. Unwanted notes that have not been signed or issued. They are usually the result of a bank changing its designs or going out of business. There are thousands of types of remaindered note for the collector to study; the catalogs devoted solely to this subject are huge.

Scyphate Coin. Coins shaped like a saucer. The Byzantine empire issued scyphate coins.

Serial Number. A number given to each bill when it is printed. No two notes have the same number. Bills are numbered in sequence (10001, 10002, 10003, etc).

Stamped Notes. Paper money to which stamps have been added to increase the value.

Star Notes. Notes that have been issued to replace damaged or misprinted notes. The serial number is followed by an asterisk.

Uniface. A coin with a portrait, emblem, or other design on only one of its two faces.

SOME USEFUL ADDRESSES

Australia. The Numismatic Association of Australia, Box 1920R, GPO Melbourne, Victoria 3001, Australia.

Canada. Canadian Numismatic Association, Box 226, Barrie, Ontario, Canada L4M 4T2

Great Britain. Royal Numismatic Society, Department of Coins & Medals, British Museum, London, England WC1B 3DG.

India. Numismatic Society of India, PO Box Hindu University, Varanasi, India 221-005.

New Zealand. Royal Numismatic Society of New Zealand, GPO Box 2023, Wellington, New Zealand.

South Africa. The South African Numismatic Society, PO Box 1689, Cape Town 8000, South Africa.

United States. The American Numismatic Association. The Secretary, ANA, Box 2366, Colorado Springs, CO 80901, USA.

United States. The American Numismatic Society, Broadway at 156th Street, New York, New York 10032, USA.

MAPS

The maps on these four pages show the places whose governments issue coins and banknotes, and what the unit of currency is. You will find more details about the currencies of these countries in a coin catalog. From time to time the list of currency-issuing countries changes: some change their names, and new ones are added to the list as they become indepedent from larger countries. For example, the Baltic states of Latvia, Lithuania, and Estonia regained their independence from the former Soviet Union in 1990 and 1991. (In catalogs, the U.S.S.R. is usually listed under Russia.) Also, many currency-issuing countries have become part of other countries or even ceased to exist. In the Middle East, the Yemen Arab Republic (which issued the riyal) and the People's Democratic Republic of Yemen (which used the dinar) have merged as the Republic of Yemen, whose currency is the riyal. A country that no longer exists is the U.S.S.R. (the Soviet Union).

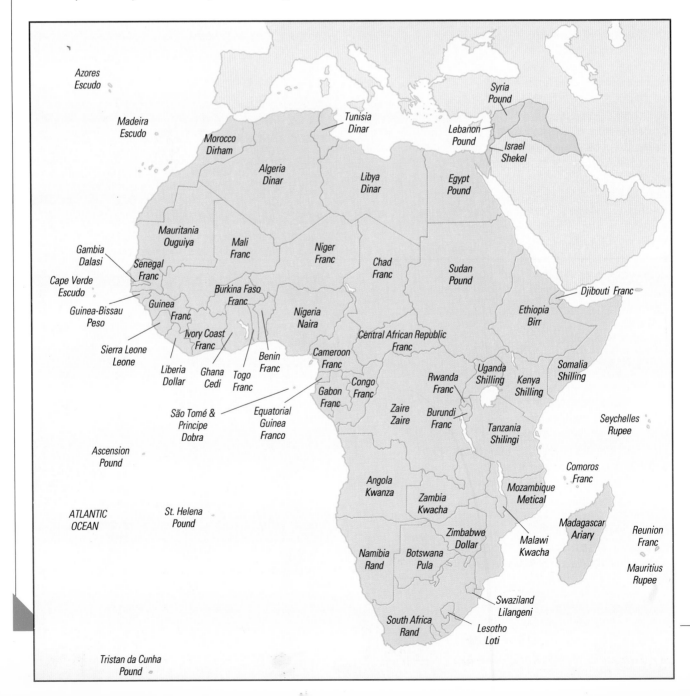

Greenland
Danish Krone

Canada
Dollar

United States of America
Dollar

St. Pierre & Miquelon
Franc

Bermuda
Dollar

ATLANTIC OCEAN

Mexico
Peso

Belize
Dollar

Cuba
Peso

Turks & Caicos Islands
Dollar

Dominican Republic
Peso

Honduras
Lempira

Guatemala
Quetzal

Haiti
Gourde

Guyana
Dollar

El Salvador
Colón

Suriname
Gulden

Venezuela
Bolivar

French Guiana
Franc

PACIFIC OCEAN

Nicaragua
Cordoba

Costa Rica
Colón

Panama
Balboa

Colombia
Peso

Ecuador
Sucre

Peru
Inti

Brazil
Cruzado

Bolivia
Peso

Paraguay
Guaraní

Argentina
Peso

Uruguay
Peso

Chile
Peso

Falkland Islands
Pound

Bahamas
Dollar

British Virgin
Islands
Dollar

St. Kitts & Nevis
Dollar

United States Virgin
Islands
Dollar

Anguilla
Dollar

Antigua &
Barbuda
Dollar

Puerto Rico
Dollar

Martinique
Franc

Cayman
Islands
Dollar

Dominica Dollar

Jamaica
Dollar

Haiti
Gourde

Dominican Republic
Peso

Montserrat
Dollar

Guadeloupe Franc

St. Vincent Dollar

St. Lucia Dollar

Aruba
Florin

Grenada
Dollar

Barbados
Dollar

Netherlands Antilles
Gulden

Trinidad &
Tobago
Dollar

73

ATLANTIC OCEAN

Iceland
Króna

Byelorussia/Belarus?
Ukraine ?

Finland
Markka

Norway
Krone

Isle of Man
Pound

Sweden
Krona

Estonia
Kroon

Latvia
Lat

Denmark
Krone

Lithuania
Lita

Russia Ruble

Netherlands
Gulden

Ireland
Punt

United
Kingdom
Pound

Germany
Mark

Poland
Zloty

Alderney Pound

Belgium
Franc

Guernsey Pound

Liechtenstein
Franc

Czechoslovakia
Koruna

Jersey Pound

Luxembourg Franc

Austria
Schilling

France
Franc

Switzerland
Franc

Hungary
Forint

Romania
Leu

Italy
Lira

Slovenia
Tolarjev

Andorra Diner

San
Marino
Lira

Croatia
Kuna

Yugoslavia
Dinar

Bulgaria
Lev

Monaco
Franc

Portugal
Escudo

Spain
Peseta

Albania
Lek

Vatican City
Lira

Greece
Drachma

Turkey
Lira

Gibraltar
Pound

Malta
Pound

MEDITERRANEAN SEA

Cyprus Pound

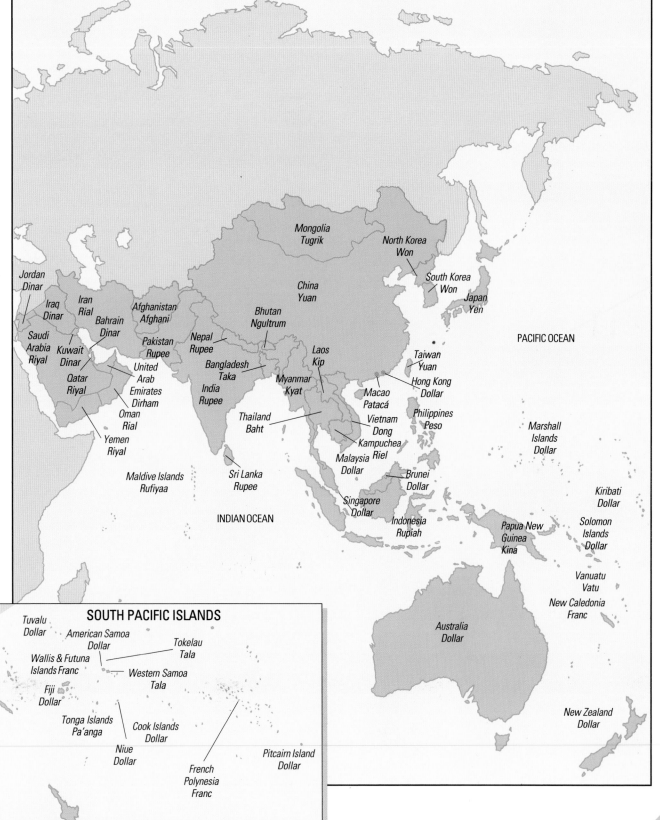

PACIFIC OCEAN

Mongolia
Tugrik

North Korea
Won

South Korea
Won

Japan
Yen

China
Yuan

Taiwan
Yuan

Hong Kong
Dollar

Jordan
Dinar

Iran
Rial

Iraq
Dinar

Afghanistan
Afghani

Bahrain
Dinar

Bhutan
Ngultrum

Saudi
Arabia
Riyal

Kuwait
Dinar

Pakistan
Rupee

Nepal
Rupee

Laos
Kip

Qatar
Riyal

United
Arab
Emirates
Dirham

Bangladesh
Taka

India
Rupee

Myanmar
Kyat

Macao
Patacá

Philippines
Peso

Marshall
Islands
Dollar

Oman
Rial

Thailand
Baht

Vietnam
Dong

Yemen
Riyal

Kampuchea
Riel

Malaysia
Dollar

Brunei
Dollar

Kiribati
Dollar

Maldive Islands
Rufiyaa

Sri Lanka
Rupee

Singapore
Dollar

Solomon
Islands
Dollar

INDIAN OCEAN

Indonesia
Rupiah

Papua New
Guinea
Kina

Vanuatu
Vatu

New Caledonia
Franc

Australia
Dollar

New Zealand
Dollar

SOUTH PACIFIC ISLANDS

Tuvalu
Dollar

American Samoa
Dollar

Tokelau
Tala

Wallis & Futuna
Islands Franc

Western Samoa
Tala

Fiji
Dollar

Tonga Islands
Pa'anga

Cook Islands
Dollar

Niue
Dollar

French
Polynesia
Franc

Pitcairn Island
Dollar

INDEX

Italic figures refer to captions or illustration labels.